D0995572

Good Housekeeping

ESSENTIAL
MICROWAVE HANDBOOK

Good Housekeeping
ESSENTIAL
MICROWAVE HANDBOOK

All you need to know to make the most of your machine,
with over 100 recipes

EBURY PRESS
LONDON

First published in 1996

1 3 5 7 9 10 8 6 4 2

Text copyright © 1996 Random House UK Limited or
The National Magazine Company Limited

All rights reserved. No part of this publication may be
reproduced, stored in a retrieval system, or transmitted in any
form or by any means, electronic, mechanical, photocopying,
recording or otherwise, without the prior permission of the
copyright owners.

The expression GOOD HOUSEKEEPING as used in the title
of this book is the trade mark of The National Magazine
Company Limited and The Hearst Corporation, registered in
the principal countries of the world, and is the absolute
property of The National Magazine Company Limited and
The Hearst Corporation. The use of this trade mark other than
with the express permission of The National Magazine
Company or The Hearst Corporation is strictly prohibited.

First published in the United Kingdom in 1996 by Ebury Press
Random House, 20 Vauxhall Bridge Road, London SW1V
2SA

Random House Australia (Pty) Limited
20 Alfred Street, Milsons Point, Sydney, New South Wales
2061, Australia

Random House New Zealand Limited
18 Poland Road, Glenfield, Auckland 10, New Zealand

Random House South Africa (Pty) Limited
PO Box 337, Bergvlei, South Africa

Random House UK Limited Reg. No. 954009

A catalogue record for this book is available from the British
Library.

ISBN 0 09 181411 1

Editor: Jennie Shapter
Design: Paul Wood
New recipes and text: Janet Warren

Printed and bound in Great Britain by
BPC Books Limited

Contents

Introduction

ALL ABOUT MICROWAVES

The microwave cooker is a remarkably efficient piece of kitchen equipment, but as with all pieces of kitchen equipment it has to be used correctly to obtain the best results. New cooking skills have to be learnt to ensure food is cooked successfully the microwave way.

Cooking with a microwave oven should be fun. Inevitably there will be disasters but hopefully not too many as this handbook is designed to take the guesswork out of microwave cooking. Also just because this piece of kitchen equipment is often called an oven don't only compare it with food cooked in the conventional oven. It is much more versatile as you will discover going through the pages of this book.

HOW IT WORKS

Microwave energy is produced by the magnetron which is a component housed inside the microwave cooker but invisible to the user. Once inside the oven this energy is used in three different ways:-

Absorbed Heat:- Microwaves are absorbed by food and liquid but they only penetrate food to a depth of 4-5 cm (1½-2 inches) so for large containers or joints the centre will be cooked by conduction hence 'standing' time is included in many of the recipes.

Reflected Heat:- The inside of most microwave cookers are metal or plastic coated metal so the waves can be reflected onto the food from all over the oven cavity.

Transmitted Heat:- Microwaves are attracted by water, fat and sugar molecules that can be found inside food. These molecules are then vibrated by the microwave energy at such a fast rate that they create heat which is transmitted to the food. Just as we can create heat if we rub our hands together.

SAFETY

Microwaves are short wavelengths similar to radio waves and should not be associated with x-rays or gamma rays. They only cause a change in temperature and not a chemical change so are quite safe.

Even so all microwaves are built to an extremely high standard and only operate when the door is closed. The door is fitted with special locks, seals and safety cut-out switches which prevent the production of microwaves should the door go out of alignment for any reason.

When you select your microwave cooker check it carries the CE mark which means it conforms to EC regulations (BS EN 60335-2-25) and also the BEAB (British Electro-technical Approvals Board) mark. This confirms the model has been tested randomly and regularly for electrical safety and microwave leakage.

It is advisable to take care to keep the door seal and hinges clean and avoid leaning on the door or banging it shut. Most manufacturers recommend that your model should be checked on a regular basis (usually every 1-2 years) to ensure everything is functioning correctly. Never attempt to repair a microwave cooker if damaged. Always contact a qualified engineer.

Finally never switch on the microwave cooker when there is nothing in it. The waves will bounce around the empty cavity and could damage the magnetron. If there are young children around who may be tempted to fiddle with the controls and accidentally start the microwave it is wise to get into the habit of keeping a glass of water in the oven when it is not in use so that the microwaves can be attracted to it should it be accidently switched on.

Note: Certain types of cardiac pacemakers can be affected by microwaves. If you know of someone who has a pacemaker fitted it is wise to seek medical advice concerning the use of the microwave when they are around.

TYPES OF MICROWAVE COOKER

There is a wide choice and variety of microwave cookers ranging from basic machines that just cook at one temperature or can be used for defrosting to highly sophisticated ovens that have extra features. These range from built-in grills, so food can be easily browned, to sensor controls where at the press of a button the oven determines the length of time and power the food to be cooked requires.

Microwave cookers are available as free standing, built-in / built-under models or feature as the second oven to a conventional cooker. A free standing model is usually sited on a work top, or it can be placed on a trolley, sideboard or even wall mounted.

Built-in microwave cookers may be sited above or below a conventional oven or somewhere else in the kitchen. Just ensure you choose a position that will not block the vent on the cooker as this allows moisture to escape from the oven while it is in use. Make sure the position is comfortable for you to check or stir the food.

MICROWAVE COOKER FEATURES

Automatic Timer:- As with the conventional cooker a delay start clock is built into the microwave so it can be programmed to switch on and off automatically.

Memories:- This allows you to programme the cooker to cook the food at several different power settings one after the other without assistance from you. It is very useful when a dish requires defrosting, reheating or cooking and then a standing time. All three times and power levels can be programmed into the cooker in one sequence and then the oven can be left to follow the programme while you do something else.

Probe:- This is a long skewer-like object that plugs into the inside of the oven. The tip of the probe is sensitive to heat so food and drink can be heated in the microwave to a set temperature. It is very useful when roasting meat as it can give an accurate reading of the inside temperature of the joint.

Sensor Control:- With this feature, seemingly like magic, the microwave eliminates all the guesswork that can be involved when trying to calculate the cooking time for certain foods. An electronic sensory processor automatically adjusts the cooking time and power level of the microwave. The control panel has settings for food types, such as meat portions, flans, vegetables, fish etc. so the food is simply placed in the oven, the appropriate setting is selected and the oven takes over cooking the food.

Touch Control:- This control panel is operated by touch which makes it easy to use and very accurate as you can programme in exactly the time required down to the last second. Also the flat facial panel with no knobs etc. is very easy to keep clean.

Variable Power:- A microwave with variable power levels lets you adjust the microwave energy output to suit the food being cooked thus giving better and more even results. Most models cook on HIGH and DEFROST which is 30% of the power output. However with variable power there are often up to 10 levels ranging from 10% of the output right through to 100%.

Shelf:- In the more sophisticated microwave cooker models there is a removable shelf unit made of either glass or metal struts. It means more dishes can be cooked in the oven at one time but don't forget that the more food in the oven the longer the cooking time.

Grill Element:- This feature is designed to overcome the problem of food not browning in the microwave. An electric element is fitted into the roof of the cooker and should the food require a brown surface then the element can be switch on.

Combination:- A microwave oven combined with a convection cooker which means you gain the speed from the microwave energy but the food when cooked has the appearance we expect from dishes straight from the conventional cooker.

Turntable/Stirrer:- In order to spread the microwaves around as evenly as possible some models come supplied with a turntable which turns the food as it cooks in its container so that it is exposed to as much penetration as possible. Other models have built-in stirrers which circulate the microwave around the food - like the magnetron they are invisible to the user.

Light:- All models come with an interior light which remains on during cooking and allows you to view the food through the door.

THE ADVANTAGES OF MICROWAVE COOKING

Speed:- A microwave cooker heats food at an incredible speed. It reduces cooking times on average to a third of that required in the conventional cooker - a real boon when time is short.

Efficient:- All domestic microwave cookers run off a 13 amp socket outlet. The microwaves only heat the molecules in the food and not the air inside the oven, so there is minimal wasted energy. Also because microwave energy cannot pass through metal, and the walls of the microwave oven are made of metal, no heat is lost outside the cavity.

Nutrition:- As the food is cooked in the minimum of water most of the taste and the nutritional value is maintained, the food also keeps its colour extremely well.

Smell Free:- When the microwave oven is in use it is almost a sealed unit so very few smells penetrate into the kitchen and also very little heat, making it an ideal piece of kitchen equipment to use during the summer.

Clean:- With microwave cooking because the majority of foods are cooked covered, there is very little risk of food splattering and burning on the cooker walls. Also the cooker walls do not become hot in the way that the surfaces of a conventional cooker do so even for the few foods that are cooked uncovered the problem is minimal.

Less Washing Up:- It is often possible to microwave food in a serving container or on the plate from which it is to be eaten. This reduces the amount and kind of washing up to a minimum.

Thawing:- Microwave ovens are very quick and efficient at thawing out foods, which makes the necessity of taking the meal out of the freezer the day before it is required a thing of the past. Also unexpected visitors can be entertained with very little fuss and effort. A plate of small cakes can be thawed in minutes.

MICROWAVE COOKING UTENSILS

Many utensils that are already in use in your kitchen are suitable for microwave cooking although there are some materials that can't be used because they deflect the microwaves. The ones to avoid are those made of metal, e.g. tins, baking trays, foil containers, foil lined dishes, china with gold or silver trim and don't forget cut glass as it contains lead.

A simple test to ascertain the suitability of a container is: Place the dish in the oven. Stand a glass bowl or jug containing 250ml (8 fl oz) cold water beside it and heat on HIGH for 1 minute. The water should be warm and the dish or container cool. If the dish or container is warm it is not advisable to use it in the microwave as it may overheat and break and also the food will not cook satisfactorily.

I suggest initially you use the equipment you already have to hand, add to it extra pieces such as a roasting rack and browning dish (see page 10) once you are more confident with the microwave method of cooking and how it can be involved in your everyday food preparation and cooking.

Consider the following points when selecting suitable microwave cookware:-

● The most efficient and suitable containers are those which allow the microwave energy to pass straight through so all the energy heats the food and not the dish.

● Regular shaped dishes are the best. An oval or square dish will not cook as evenly as a round one as the food at each end or in the corners is subjected to more microwave energy and so will cook more quickly than the rest of the food.

● Straight sided dishes are better than sloping ones.

● A large shallow dish in which the food is spread out evenly will cook more efficiently than a deep one.

● Ring moulds are particularly good as they allow microwaves to reach the food surface from the inner ring as well as the outside. If you don't own a ring mould you can make one by placing a glass tumbler in the centre of a round container.

● Avoid dishes, plates, cups or jugs repaired with glue - the glue could melt in the heat.

● Consider that some foods as they cook, boil up, so ideally no food should come more than two-thirds up the sides of it container when it is put in to the oven to cook.

SUITABLE CONTAINER MATERIALS

China and Pottery:- Standard glazed household china and pottery can be used except those with a metal decorative design and don't forget to check the base in case there is a signature. If, however, you are unsure over the suitability of a certain piece of pottery then follow the test on page 8. Unglazed china and pottery is porous and therefore absorbs moisture which attracts microwaves into the material and away from the food. This can be an advantage when cooking cheaper cuts of meat as they cook the meat more slowly therefore rendering it more tender. Unglazed chicken and fish bricks are good for long slow cooking. Soak them well first and if they dry out add more warm water. If cold water is added the brick could crack.

Glassware and Glass Ceramic:- Ovenproof glass and glass ceramic dishes are perhaps the most suitable microwave cookware. Many of them such as measuring jugs and mixing bowls are useful in the early stages of food preparation then the actual dishes double as serving dishes so saving on the washing up.

Paper:- Paper plates, kitchen paper and paper napkins can all be used in the microwave for short term reheating tasks. If using paper plates they should be white (any colour might transfer to the food) and uncoated (wax and plastic coatings might melt). Absorbent kitchen paper and napkins (not made from recycled paper as it may contain metal fragments) are useful to absorb moisture such as under bread or pastries to prevent them becoming soggy and they can also be used as a loose covering on foods such as bacon to contain any splashing.

Plastics:- As a rough guide, rigid plastics are usually safe in a microwave while soft ones are not. Unless you are using a plastic that is guaranteed microwave safe do the water test on page 8. Note that Melamine absorbs microwaves and prevents food cooking. Look out for the large selection of rigid plastic microwave cookware available nowadays. Many are quite attractive and will double up as serving dishes. They can also be used in the freezer with sealing lids specially supplied for the purpose. Plastic wrap (microwave food wrap) is excellent for covering the food as it cooks in the microwave but remember either a corner should be turned back or the film should be pierced to allow for the release of steam and to prevent the wrap billowing up and then collapsing and sticking to the food.

Wood, Wicker or Straw Baskets:- All can be used for brief periods of reheating but will dry out and crack if exposed to microwave energy for too long. Bread rolls are ideal if placed in a small basket lined with a paper napkin. If wood is used in the microwave and it appears to be drying out then recondition the wood with a light coating of vegetable oil, rubbed in well.

MICROWAVE ACCESSORIES

More and more accessories are becoming available for specific use in the microwave but again as with cooking utensils it is best to buy them gradually when you have gauged how best the microwave can be used for your particular style of cooking.

Browning Dish or Skillet:- Made of specially coated ceramic for searing and colouring foods that would otherwise be grilled or fried. Not essential if you have a grill or combination cooker.

Defrosting Rack:- Comes with a built-in drip tray and is excellent for defrosting meat as it prevents the joint sitting in its own juices.

Plate Stackers/Vented Plate Covers:- Specially designed clear plastic rings that enable two plates to be stacked one on top of the other for reheating. The top plate is either covered loosely with microwave food wrap or alternatively a vented plate cover is used which can be washed and then used again.

Roasting Rack - Has a ridged surface which allows microwaves to circulate all round the food and prevents foods like joints of meat sitting in their own juices or fat as they cook.

Thermometer:- A specially designed microwave thermometer can be inserted into meat or poultry while it is cooking so you can continually check at what stage it is at. It works on the same principle as the probe but as it is not linked into the microwave it cannot control how the joint is cooked.

MICROWAVE TERMS AND TECHNIQUES

As with all different types of cooking there are different techniques and methods that need to be mastered and understood.

Arrangement of Food:- To ensure food is thawed, reheated or cooked evenly it must be arranged correctly. Place thicker or more dense items towards the edges of the dish so they are nearer the source of the microwaves with thinner, more delicate items near the centre.

When arranging individual items such as small cakes, jacket potatoes or baked apples arrange them in a circle on a plate or directly on the oven turntable or shelf. Check the items as they thaw, reheat or cook moving them around if necessary so they are all evenly exposed to the microwave energy.

The more surface area that can be exposed to the microwaves the quicker and more even the thawing, reheating or cooking will be.

Browning:- The standard microwave cooker does not brown food very well although joints of meat or poultry that require more than 20 minutes cooking do brown slightly but they will not be crisp and will look different from conventionally cooked dishes.

Small items of meat such as chops, beefburgers etc. can be cooked on a browning dish. Other ways of giving savoury food a more traditionally browned appearance is to sprinkle over paprika pepper, browned breadcrumbs, or brush the surface with brown, tomato, Tabasco, soy or Worcestershire sauce or glaze with honey, apricot jam or marmalade.

Cakes and pastries made with brown flour and sugar look more pleasing to the eye and dishes can always be placed under the grill, just before serving, when a brown and crisp surface is required.

Covering:- Foods that need to be kept moist during cooking should be covered not only to prevent the food from drying out but also by keeping most of the steam and heat in, the food cooks more quickly.

The cover can be of any material that is suitable for use in a microwave cooker. If microwave food wrap, a plastic bag, boil-in-the-bag or roasting bag is used make a slit or hole in it to prevent ballooning, bursting or sticking to the food. It will also allow steam to escape. When using a lid do not cover the dish completely as again some steam has to be allowed to escape. Take care when removing either a rigid lid or microwave food wrap. Always open it away from you as there will be a gush of hot, moist air that can cause a nasty scald.

Fatty foods such as bacon rashers should be covered with a sheet of kitchen paper as this absorbs the fat and contains any spits and so keeps the cooker clean.

Shielding:- Certain foods will require shielding to protect them from overcooking. A very small piece of foil, shiny side inside, is wrapped closely around the food. Take care not to use too much foil at any one time as it could damage the magnetron.

Standing Time:- Once the microwave programme has finished the microwave energy inside the food continues to cook. When a recipe states 'standing' time this is to complete the cooking time. The more dense the food e.g. a joint of meat, the longer the 'standing' time.

Stirring:- The reason for stirring foods as they cook in the microwave is to ensure the heat is evenly distributed. When a dish such as a casserole is placed in the microwave either to reheat or cook, the outside edges heat up first because microwave energy only penetrates to a depth of 4-5 cm (1½-2 inches). Consequently if the food is stirred several times during cooking, from the outside in towards the centre, then the heat is more evenly distributed.

Starting Time:- This really applies to all cooking, if the food comes straight from the fridge then obviously it will take longer to cook than if it starts at room temperature.

Seasoning:- Salt draws out moisture and has a toughening effect on fish, meat and vegetables so do not add salt directly to foods without liquid until after they are cooked. As microwave cooking is so quick there is not enough time for the flavour of seasonings and herbs to be absorbed thoroughly into the food. Season lightly initially then adjust the taste at the end of the cooking time.

THAWING

The facility to defrost food rapidly and efficiently in the microwave is extremely useful and dispenses with the need to plan ahead. Many microwave cookers have a defrost control which takes care of thawing food automatically but if your oven is not fitted with one, gentle thawing can be accomplished easily. Depending on the size and density of the item to be defrosted switch the power on for short 30 second to 1 minute bursts then leave the food to 'stand' for 30 seconds to 1 minute between each burst. When food is thawed smaller ice crystals will melt first followed by larger ones. Therefore if thawing is too rapid the parts of food with the smallest ice crystals or the thinner parts will start to cook before the rest of the food has thawed.

Tips for Successful Thawing:-

● Loosely cover most foods with microwave food wrap when defrosting. The exception are baked foods such as cakes, bread and pastry which are best placed on a piece of absorbent kitchen paper.

● Any large lumps of ice should be removed from the food before it is thawed.

● Unless the microwave cooker has a turntable keep rearranging the food so the microwave energy effects all parts of the food evenly.

● A frozen block of food such as a casserole or soup should closely fit the container in which it is being thawed otherwise the edges of the defrosting food will spread and overheat before the main bulk of the food has started to thaw.

● When defrosting liquid based foods such as soups and casseroles, as the cycle progresses, use a fork to try and break up the partially frozen food and stir it occasionally so it thaws as evenly as possible. This also applies to frozen minced meat as it thaws.

● Items such as pastry or fruit are best only partially thawed in the microwave then left at room temperature to finish the process otherwise the items can easily start cooking if defrosted for too long.

● If any parts of the food appears to be starting to cook during defrosting cover them with small pieces of foil, shiny side inside, so they are protected.

● Replace metal ties on polythene bags with string or plastic ties and transfer food from aluminium foil trays into more suitable containers.

● An approximate guide to thawing a selection of food is given on pages 117-122. The temperature of frozen foods can vary so always underestimate thawing time and take into account the thawing that will take place during the final standing time.

REHEATING

Reheating food in the microwave is so easy and there is very little loss of colour or nutrients and very little risk of the food drying up. Meals can be reheated as and when they are required on the serving plate so saving on the washing up. Also because the reheating process in the microwave is so quick harmful germs have less chance to survive making it a much safer process.

Tips for Successful Reheating:-

● If possible reheat food at room temperature, if it comes straight from the fridge then obviously it will need longer in the microwave to reach the required temperature.

● Cover food either with a lid or microwave food wrap while reheating.

● The arrangement of the food is important. Dense or thicker items of food should be arranged nearer the edges of the plate. When reheating a plated meal and for casserole type dishes arrange the food evenly.

● Stir soups, casseroles, sauces etc. during reheating to help distribute the heat as evenly as possible.

● Stand moist items such as cakes, bread and pastries on absorbent paper so they do not become too soggy.

● Be very careful when reheating small pastry pies or jam filled doughnuts. Although the outside may seem just warm the filling will probably be very hot so it is advisable to leave the items to 'stand' for a few minutes so the heat can disperse.

● It is best to underestimate the reheating time, then add more if necessary. Overheating dries and toughens many foods.

● One plate of food covered with microwave food wrap and from room temperature should take about 3-4 minutes to reheat. To test if it is ready feel the centre bottom of the plate, if it is warm then the food is ready.

CLEANING

Cleaning of the microwave is very easy but very essential if the oven is to work efficiently. If particles of grease and dirt are allowed to build up within it then the microwave energy is attracted to the splashes as well as the food being cooked and the cooking process will be slowed down.

Get into the habit of cleaning out the interior of the microwave oven and around the door seal either at the end of every day or after each use. All that is needed is a wipe round with a warm, damp cloth wrung out of a mild detergent solution. If any splashes have been allowed to build up and they are difficult to remove then place a small bowl of water mixed with a few drops of lemon juice into the microwave and heat it to boiling point. This will produce steam which condenses on the interior surfaces and softens any deposits; incidentally this process can also be used to remove any strong odours from inside the cavity.

Do not use abrasive cleaners which could damage the

interior surface and never use a knife or sharp object to scrape off deposits. Your manufacturer's handbook will give detailed advice on cleaning and suitable products.

Removable parts such as turntables and shelves can either be washed up in the normal way in the sink or if they are suitable put into the dishwasher.

HINTS AND TIPS

A microwave oven has so many other uses than just for the cooking of meals. Here are just a few of the many ways in which it can help in food preparation.

Chocolate:- Place 25 g (1 oz) chocolate in a heatproof bowl and heat on HIGH for 1-2 minutes until shiny. Remove and stir until smooth.

Butter:- To soften butter place about 125 g (4 oz) in a non-foil wrapper and heat on LOW for 30-40 seconds until spreadable.

Syrup and Honey:- To restore the texture of syrup or honey that has crystallised microwave it in the jar on HIGH for about 1 minute.

Toasted Nuts, Seeds and Coconut:- Spread out on a heatproof plate or shallow dish and microwave on HIGH for 3-8 minutes depending on the amount and type. Stir the ingredients often so they brown evenly.

Blanching Almonds:- Heat 300 ml (½ pint) water in a heatproof bowl, add 125g (4 oz) almonds, heat on HIGH for 1 minute, drain, cool then slip off the skins, dry and use as required.

Roasting Chestnuts:- Slit the skins with a sharp knife or pair of scissors and microwave on HIGH for 2-3 minutes per 225 g (8 oz).

Hazelnuts:- To remove the skins and brown hazelnuts arrange in a single layer between two sheets of kitchen paper. Microwave on HIGH for 30 seconds to 1 minute, then rub off the skins. Return the nuts to the oven this time uncovered. Continue to cook on HIGH until golden brown, turning them often so they brown evenly.

Dried Fruit:- To soften dried fruit place in a heatproof bowl, cover with water and heat on HIGH for 4 minutes. Stir, leave to 'stand' for 5 minutes then drain well, dry and use as required.

Softening Sugar:- If sugar has become hard in its original wrapping soften it on HIGH for 30 seconds.

Caramelise Sugar:- Put 175 g (6 oz) sugar into a 1 litre (1¾ pint) heatproof jug. Mix in 60 ml (4 tbsp) water. Cook on HIGH for 5-6 minutes, without stirring, until golden. The caramel will continue to cook after it has been removed from the oven, so stop when still only light golden.

Gelatine:- In a small heatproof bowl sprinkle gelatine over measured liquid. Allow to stand for 1 minute then heat on HIGH for 1-2 minutes, stirring until dissolved. Do not allow the liquid to boil.

Poppadoms:- Brush poppadoms lightly with oil. Place one at a time on absorbent kitchen paper on the turntable or oven floor for models without a turntable. Heat on HIGH for 1 minute, or until crisp, turning once.

Croûtons:- Melt 25 g (1 oz) butter in a shallow heatproof dish. Remove the crusts from two thick slices of bread and cut into small cubes. Toss in the fat then return the dish, uncovered, to the cooker and heat on HIGH for 3-4 minutes, stirring several times so the croûtons brown evenly. Leave to cool on absorbent paper.

Sterilising Jam Jars:- Half fill each jar with water and microwave on HIGH for 2 minutes or until water is boiling. Carefully remove the jars - they will be hot - pour off the water and drain upside down for a few minutes before drying with a clean tea towel and filling.

Baby Bottles:- To warm up a baby's bottle of milk, place it in the microwave without lid or teat and warm on MEDIUM for 1-2 minutes. Test the temperature in the normal way before giving it to baby.

Porridge:- Mix 45 ml (3 tbsp) porridge oats in a cereal bowl with 150 ml (¼ pint) water. Microwave uncovered on HIGH for 2-3 minutes. Add a pinch of salt, stir well, then leave to 'stand' for 1-2 minutes before serving with milk, and sugar or golden syrup.

THE RECIPES

All the recipes in this book have been tested in a 850W microwave cooker.

The power levels used in this book are:-

HIGH-850 watts
MEDIUM-HIGH-650 watts
MEDIUM-450 watts
DEFROST or MEDIUM LOW-300 watts
LOW-150 watts

If your cooker has a lower power output then adjust the thawing, reheating and cooking times as follows. When calculating the time always start with the shortest amount. More time can always be added if necessary but once the food is overcooked there is nothing that can be done:-

700 watt oven - add approximately 10-15 seconds per minute.
600 watt oven - add approximately 15-20 seconds per minute.
500 watt oven - add approximately 20-25 seconds per minute

Adapting your Favourite Recipes

Once you feel confident with microwave cookery you can start to adapt your family's favourite recipes that are suitable for microwave cooking. Use the following guidelines:-

● Try and find a similar recipe in your microwave cookbook to use as a guide.

● Start with a quarter of the conventional cooking time then add more as necessary.

● Reduce the liquid content of casserole by about a quarter as there is less evaporation when cooking in the microwave.

● Conversely when cooking cake type mixture the liquid content should be increased by about a half.

● Use a deeper dish than in the conventional method, food cooking in the microwave oven is more likely to bubble over.

● Always use less seasoning initially then adjust the taste before serving.

● Smaller quantities cook fastest in the microwave so keep to a maximum of 6 servings at any one time.

SOUPS AND STARTERS

Microwave ovens can be used to cook soups from fresh ingredients that would take much longer if cooked conventionally as well as for thawing and reheating soups that have already been made. The microwave oven can also be used just for heating canned or dehydrated soups.

Always select a dish, in which to cook the soup, that allows plenty of room for the liquid to expand and also for it to be stirred. Stirring of the soup during cooking is important so it reaches an even temperature. Invariably the edges of the soup will be hot and start to bubble long before the centre reaches the same temperature.

If time permits make soup in the microwave the day before it is required so the flavours develop as the soup is left to stand.

TO THAW AND/OR REHEAT READY PREPARED SOUP

CANNED DILUTED:
Put the soup straight into soup bowl and microwave on
HIGH: 1 bowl - 3 minutes
            2 bowls - 7 minutes
Stir the soup halfway through the cooking time, then leave to **STAND** for 1-2 minutes before serving.

CANNED UNDILUTED:
Put the soup into a 1 litre (1¾ pint) basin or microwave-proof jug. Mix in the milk or water as directed on the can. Cover and heat on **HIGH** for 5 minutes.
Stir the soup so the heat is evenly distributed then leave covered to **STAND** for 2-3 minutes before serving.

PACKET:
 In a large bowl or jug blend the soup mix with the liquid as directed on the packet. Cover and cook on
HIGH for 7 minutes stirring once or twice. Leave the soup to **STAND** for 2 minutes before serving.

FROZEN:
Defrost the soup in a microwave-proof bowl on
MEDIUM-LOW or DEFROST:
            1 litre(1¾ pints) - 12 minutes
            600 ml (1 pint) - 6 minutes
            300 ml (½ pint) - 4 minutes
Break the soup apart with a fork as it thaws.

REHEAT THAWED SOUP:
Keep the soup still in the same bowl and reheat on
MEDIUM-HIGH:
            1 litre (1¾ pints) - 10 minutes
            600 ml (1 pint) - 9 minutes
            300 ml (½ pint) - 6 minutes
As the soup reheats stir the liquid twice.

Bouillabaisse

Traditional bouillabaisse is made with varieties of fish only available in the South of France. However, regional variations, use whatever fish is available locally. Traditionally the fish is removed from the soup and served on a separate plate.

Preparation time: 30 minutes, plus soaking
Cooking time: 18-19 minutes
Cals per serving: 320-210
Serves 4-6

few strands saffron	**2 garlic cloves**
900 g (2 lb) mixed fish and shellfish eg monkfish, red mullet and cooked, shelled Mediterranean prawns, cleaned	**1 bay leaf**
	2.5 ml (½ tsp) fennel seeds
2 medium onions	**finely shredded rind of ½ orange**
1 celery stick	**salt and pepper**
60 ml (4 tbsp) olive oil	**900 ml (1½ pints) hot fish stock**
4 plum tomatoes, skinned	**TO GARNISH**
	parsley sprigs

1 Put the saffron into a small bowl, pour in 150 ml (¼ pint) boiling water and leave to soak for 30 minutes. Skin and fillet the fish if necessary, then cut into fairly large, thick pieces.

2 Peel and slice the onions. Chop the celery and place in a large microwave casserole dish with the onions and olive oil. Microwave on HIGH for 8 minutes, stirring 2-3 times.

3 Slice the tomatoes, peel and crush the garlic and add to the casserole dish with the bay leaf, fennel seeds, orange rind, seasoning, stock and saffron liquid. Cover and microwave on HIGH for 5 minutes.

4 Add the fish, re-cover and microwave on HIGH for 4 minutes.

5 Stir in the prawns, re-cover and cook on HIGH for 1-2 minutes, until soup is boiling and fish are cooked but still holding their shape. Serve in warmed soup bowls, garnished with parsley and accompanied by French bread.

VARIATION
For a less expensive alternative, use cod or other firm white fish, to replace the mixed fish and shellfish.

Tomato and Pepper Soup

Tomato soup is always very popular. This version also includes red pepper to make it extra special in both flavour and colour.

Preparation time: 10 minutes
Cooking time: 11-13 minutes
Cals per serving: 90
Serves 4

400 g (14 oz) can tomatoes in tomato juice	**5 ml (1 tsp) sugar**
200 g (7 oz) can pimientos, drained	**15 ml (1 tbsp) sun-dried tomato paste**
1 garlic clove	**salt and pepper**
1 small onion	**TO GARNISH**
15 ml (1 tbsp) vegetable oil	**snipped fresh chives**
15 ml (1 tbsp) plain white flour	**croûtons**
450 ml (¾ pint) chicken stock	

1 Purée the tomatoes and juice with the pimientos in a blender or food processor, then sieve to remove the seeds.

2 Peel the garlic and crush. Peel and finely chop the onion. Place the oil, garlic and onion in a large bowl, cover and microwave on HIGH for 5 minutes until starting to soften.

3 Stir in the flour then gradually blend in the stock. Add the sugar, sun-dried tomato paste, tomato and pimento purée and stir well.

4 Microwave, uncovered, on HIGH for 6-8 minutes until thickened, stirring frequently. Season with salt and pepper to taste.

5 Spoon into warmed soup bowls and serve garnished with snipped chives and croûtons (see page 13).

Lentil and Bacon Soup

The perfect soup for a chilly winter's night. The strong flavours of the bacon, lentils, carrots and leeks combine to make a thick and warming soup.

Preparation time: 15 minutes
Cooking time: 19-20 minutes
Cals per serving: 265
Serves 6

125 g (4 oz) streaky bacon, derinded	**125 g (4 oz) red lentils**
225 g (8 oz) leeks	**1.6 litres (2¾ pints) chicken stock**
350 g (12 oz) carrots	**salt and pepper**
25 g (1 oz) butter or margarine	**30 ml (2 tbsp) chopped fresh parsley**

1 Chop the bacon. Trim and finely chop the leeks. Peel and finely chop the carrots.

2 Put the bacon and butter in a large heatproof bowl and microwave on HIGH for 2 minutes. Add the lentils and toss them in the mixture so they are coated in the fat, then add the leeks, carrots and stock.

3 Cover and microwave on HIGH for 15 minutes until the lentils are cooked. Carefully stir the mixture two or three times during cooking.

4 Allow the soup to cool slightly, then transfer to a blender or food processor and purée until smooth.

5 Return the soup to the bowl. Season with salt and pepper to taste. Cover and microwave on HIGH for 2-3 minutes until boiling.

6 Spoon into warmed soup bowls and serve sprinkled with chopped parsley.

French Onion Soup

This tasty dark brown soup is topped with golden slices of French bread topped with melted Cheddar cheese.

Preparation time: 15 minutes
Cooking time: 30 minutes
Cals per serving: 380-250
Serves: 4-6

350 g (12 oz) onions	**5 ml (1 tsp) chopped fresh thyme**
50 g (2 oz) butter	**1 bay leaf**
5 ml (1 tsp) caster sugar	**6 slices French bread**
15 ml (1 tbsp) plain white flour	**75 g (3 oz) Cheddar cheese**
1.1 litres (2 pints) hot beef stock	**salt and pepper**

1 Peel the onions and finely slice. Place the onions, butter and sugar in a large heatproof bowl and microwave on HIGH for 20 minutes, stirring occasionally until the onions brown.

2 Stir in the flour, then gradually blend in the hot stock. Stir in the thyme and bay leaf. Cook the soup uncovered on HIGH for 10 minutes so the flavours develop.

3 Meanwhile arrange the bread slices on a grill pan and grill on one side. Turn over. Grate the cheese and sprinkle over the bread slices. Place under the grill and cook until golden brown. Place the slices of bread in the bottom of a warmed soup tureen.

4 When the soup is ready remove the bay leaf and season with salt and pepper. Pour the soup into the tureen. The bread will float to the surface and a slice is served with each portion.

Celeriac and Orange Soup

The subtle flavour of the celeriac blends well with the sharp tang of the orange in this velvety textured soup.

Preparation time: 15 minutes
Cooking time: 26 minutes
Cals per serving: 160
Serves: 6

450g (1 lb) celeriac	**salt and pepper**
225 g (8 oz) onions	**TO GARNISH**
50 g (2 oz) butter	**90 ml (6 tbsp) single cream**
2 large oranges	**paprika**
600 ml (1 pint) hot chicken stock	**snipped chives**
450 ml (¾ pint) milk	

1 Peel the celeriac and chop into 2.5 cm (1 inch) pieces. Peel and chop the onions. Place the butter in a large heatproof bowl and microwave on HIGH for 40 seconds, until butter has melted.

2 Stir in the celeriac and the onion making sure the vegetables are well coated with the butter. Using a potato peeler remove the rind only from one of the oranges and add to the vegetables in the bowl.

3 Cover the bowl and microwave on HIGH for 10 minutes, stirring the vegetables after 5 minutes.

4 Add the hot stock, re-cover and cook the soup on HIGH for a further 10 minutes or until the vegetables are tender. Remove the orange rind. Allow the soup to cool slightly, then transfer to a blender or food processor and purée until smooth.

5 Remove the rind from the remaining orange with a zester, put the pieces into a small bowl cover with water and blanch in the microwave on HIGH for 2 minutes. Drain and reserve for garnish. Squeeze the juice from both oranges.

6 Return the soup to the bowl and stir in the milk and orange juice. Season with salt and pepper to taste. Reheat on HIGH for 3 minutes until piping hot.

7 Serve in warmed soup bowls garnished with a swirl of cream, paprika, a few snipped chives and the reserved strips of orange rind.

Watercress Soup

An extremely versatile soup which is delicious served warm during the winter months, but is equally tasty served chilled as a refreshing starter to a summer meal. Serve this soup topped with a little crumbled Stilton cheese for a festive touch.

Preparation time: 10 minutes
Cooking time: 19-20 minutes
Cals per serving: 325
Serves: 6

1 large onion	**900 ml (1½ pints) chicken stock**
50 g (2 oz) butter or margarine	**300 ml (½ pint) double cream**
2 large bunches of watercress	**salt and pepper**
45 ml (3 tbsp) plain white flour	

1 Peel and chop the onion. Dice the butter and place in large heatproof bowl and microwave on HIGH for 40-60 seconds until melted. Add the onion, cover and microwave on HIGH for 5-6 minutes until softened.

2 Wash and trim the watercress. Reserve a few sprigs for garnish and chop the remainder. Stir into the onion mixture. Cover and microwave on HIGH for 2 minutes.

3 Stir in the flour then gradually blend in the stock. Re-cover and microwave on HIGH for 6 minutes, stirring frequently.

4 Allow the soup to cool for about 5 minutes then transfer to a blender or food processor and purée until smooth.

5 Return the soup to the bowl. Stir in the cream. Season with salt and pepper to taste. If serving hot, cover and microwave on LOW for about 5 minutes, stirring frequently, until hot but not boiling.

6 Spoon into warmed soup bowls and serve garnished with the reserved watercress sprigs. To serve cold, leave to cool then chill in the refrigerator for at least 1 hour.

Vichyssoise

This classic soup is made with potatoes and leeks and enriched with a little double cream and blue cheese. For a chilled summer soup replace the cream with crème fraîche and serve chilled.

Preparation time: 15 minutes
Cooking time: 27 minutes
Cals per serving: 175
Serves: 6

1 medium onion	**450 ml (¾ pint) milk**
350 g (12 oz) potatoes	**salt and freshly ground black pepper**
350 g (12 oz) leeks	**30 ml (2 tbsp) double cream**
15 ml (1 tbsp) vegetable oil	**25 g (1 oz) crumbly blue cheese, such as Stilton**
450 ml (¾ pint) chicken stock	**15 ml (1 tbsp) snipped fresh chives**

1 Peel and finely chop the onion. Peel and dice the potatoes. Trim and thinly slice the leeks. Put the oil and onion in a large heatproof bowl, cover and microwave on HIGH for 5 minutes until softened. Stir once.

2 Add the potatoes and leeks, re-cover and microwave on HIGH for 5 minutes stirring frequently.

3 Stir in the chicken stock, re-cover and microwave on HIGH for 14 minutes stirring occasionally, until the vegetables are soft.

4 Allow the soup to cool slightly, then transfer to a blender or food processor and purée until smooth.

5 Return the soup to the bowl. Stir in the milk and season with salt and pepper to taste. Cover and microwave on HIGH for 3 minutes until boiling.

6 Stir in the cream and cheese. Spoon into warmed soup bowls. Serve sprinkled with snipped chives.

Spicy Prawns

This quick to prepare starter combines cooked prawns with an exotic sauce flavoured with coriander, cumin, ginger and coconut. Poppadums are a perfect accompaniment and only take seconds in the microwave oven.

Preparation time: 10 minutes
Cooking time: 12-13 minutes
Cals per serving: 70
Serves: 6

1 small onion	**15 g (½ oz) creamed coconut**
1 garlic clove	**5 ml (1 tsp) tomato purée**
3 large tomatoes	**450 g (1 lb) cooked peeled prawns**
2.5 cm (1 inch) piece of fresh root ginger	**salt and pepper**
2.5 ml (½ tsp) ground coriander	**TO SERVE**
2.5 ml (½ tsp) ground cumin	**chopped fresh coriander**
15 ml (1 tbsp) red wine vinegar	**poppadums**

1 Peel and chop the onion and garlic. Roughly chop the tomatoes. Peel and finely grate the ginger.

2 Place the onion, garlic, tomatoes, ginger, coriander, cumin, vinegar, creamed coconut and tomato purée into a medium heatproof bowl. Cook uncovered on HIGH for 10 minutes or until thickened and reduced, stirring occasionally.

3 Stir in the prawns. Cook on HIGH for 2-3 minutes or until the prawns are heated through, stirring once.

4 Season to taste with salt and pepper, then serve hot, garnished with chopped coriander and accompanied by poppadums. (see page 13)

Aubergine Dip with Pitta Bread

A smooth and spicy dip with just a hint of chilli. It can also be served as a dip with crudités.

Preparation time: 10 minutes
Cooking time: 6½ minutes
Cals per serving: 340
Serves: 2

1 small aubergine	**150 ml (¼ pint) natural yogurt**
1 garlic clove	**salt and pepper**
15 ml (1 tbsp) olive oil	**15 ml (1 tbsp) chopped fresh parsley**
pinch of mild chilli powder	**TO SERVE**
2.5 ml (½ tsp) ground cumin	**black olives**
2.5 ml (½ tsp) ground coriander	**chopped fresh coriander**
10 ml (2 tsp) lemon juice	**2 pitta bread**

1 Wash the aubergine and prick the skin all over with a fork. Place on a plate. Microwave on HIGH for 4 minutes or until very soft when pressed with a finger. Leave to stand.

2 Meanwhile, peel and crush the garlic. Place in a medium bowl with the oil, chilli powder, cumin and coriander. Cook on HIGH for 2 minutes stirring twice. Stir in the lemon juice.

3 Cut the aubergine in half and scoop out the flesh. Add to the cooked spices and with a fork mash to a pulp. Gradually beat in the yogurt then season well with salt and pepper. Stir in the chopped parsley.

4 Spoon the aubergine dip into two individual serving bowls and garnish with black olives and coriander.

5 Heat the pitta bread on HIGH for 30 seconds or until warm. Cut into fingers and serve immediately with the aubergine dip.

Farmhouse Eggs

A popular and simple starter, these eggs are cooked with ham and tomatoes and flavoured with fresh basil. For a dinner party flash under the grill to brown the cheesy topping.

Preparation time: 5 minutes
Cooking time: 1½ minutes, plus standing
Cals per serving: 200
Serves 4

75 g (3 oz) thinly sliced ham	**30 ml (2 tbsp) chopped fresh basil**
4 eggs	**75 g (3 oz) Cheddar cheese**
4 tomato slices	**TO GARNISH**
	fresh basil sprigs

1 Lightly butter 4 ramekin dishes. Chop the ham and divide between the ramekin dishes. Break an egg into each dish on top of the ham.

2 Place a tomato slice on top of each egg and sprinkle over the basil.

3 Grate the cheese and scatter over the top of each dish. Arrange the dishes in a circle on a large plate. Microwave uncovered, on HIGH for 1 minute 30 seconds.

4 Either leave the dishes to STAND for 2 minutes so the eggs finish cooking or alternatively place them under a preheated grill to brown the cheese. The eggs will also continue to cook.

5 Serve with freshly made toast or warmed French bread and garnish each dish with a sprig of basil.

Mushrooms with Savoury Butter

Mushrooms cooked in a savoury butter are always a firm favourite. There is a choice of three savoury butters. All of these recipes will taste delicious served with French bread, to mop up the juices.

Preparation time: 15 minutes
Cooking time: 4½-5 minutes
Cals per serving: 270
Serves 2

275 g (10 oz) mixed mushrooms eg button, shiitake, chestnut or field	**15 ml (1 tbsp) chopped fresh parsley**
GARLIC BUTTER	**30 ml (2 tbsp) finely grated fresh Parmesan cheese**
2 garlic cloves	**TO GARNISH**
50 g (2 oz) butter	**4 lemon twists**
5 ml (1 tsp) finely grated lemon rind	**parsley sprigs**
salt and pepper	

1 Select three or four varieties of mushrooms and halve or quarter any large ones, so that they are all about the same size. Peel and crush the garlic.

2 Place the butter and garlic in a medium casserole dish, cover and microwave on HIGH for 2 minutes, until butter melts and garlic browns. Stir once.

3 Add the mushrooms, lemon rind and seasoning and stir to coat. Cover and microwave on HIGH for 2½-3 minutes. Stir in parsley.

4 Arrange the mushrooms on two, warmed serving plates. Sprinkle the cheese over the mushrooms. Garnish with lemon twists and parsley and serve with French bread.

VARIATIONS

Sun-dried Tomato Butter

Place 50 g (2 oz) butter and 1 small finely chopped onion in a medium casserole dish. Cover and cook on HIGH for 3 minutes, stirring twice. Stir in 15 ml (1 tbsp) sun-dried tomato paste and seasoning. Add the mushrooms and stir to coat. Cover and cook on HIGH for 2½-3 minutes. Serve garnished with 15 ml (1 tbsp) chopped coriander.

Tarragon and Hazelnut Butter

Place 50 g (2 oz) butter and 25 g (1 oz) roughly chopped hazelnuts in a medium casserole dish. Cover and cook on HIGH for 2 minutes, until lightly browned. Stir in mushrooms and seasoning. Cover and cook on HIGH for 2½-3 minutes. Stir in 15 ml (1 tbsp) chopped tarragon and serve.

Artichokes with Beurre Blanc

The tender leaves of globe artichokes, taste wonderful dipped in this sharp herb and butter sauce.

Preparation time: 15 minutes
Cooking time: 4½-5 minutes
Cals per serving: 400
Serves 2

2 whole fresh artichokes	**15 ml (1 tbsp) white wine vinegar**
30 ml (2 tbsp) lemon juice	**45 ml (3 tbsp) dry white wine**
BEURRE BLANC	**salt and pepper**
2 small shallots	**15 ml (1 tbsp) chopped fresh parsley**
100 g (4 oz) butter	**15 ml (1 tbsp) chopped fresh tarragon**

1 Trim 2.5 cm (1 inch) off the tops of the artichokes. Trim each stalk close to the base of the artichoke. Snip the tops off the outer leaves.

2 Brush all over the artichokes with lemon juice to prevent discoloration. Place in a shallow microwave dish. Add 60 ml (4 tbsp) cold water and cover with pierced microwave film.

3 Microwave on HIGH for 10 minutes, or until the artichoke bases pierce easily with a skewer. Leave to stand for 5 minutes, covered.

4 Meanwhile make the sauce. Finely chop the shallots. Cut the butter into tiny dice. Place the vinegar, white wine and shallots in a bowl and cook on HIGH for 2 minutes.

5 Whisk in the butter, until it is all absorbed. If necessary re-heat the sauce on HIGH for 15-30 seconds, if it starts to over-cool whilst whisking in the butter. Re-heat finished sauce on HIGH for 20-30 seconds, and whisk thoroughly. Do not let the sauce become too hot or the butter will become greasy. Season and stir in the chopped herbs.

6 Serve artichokes accompanied by the beurre blanc sauce.

VARIATION

If wished remove the centre leaves of the artichoke and scrape out the hairy choke. Fill the centre with the beurre blanc.

Chicken Liver Pâté

A tasty combination of chicken livers, bacon and onions flavoured with green peppercorns, mustard, brandy and garlic. It is particularly good served with toasted wholemeal bread.

Preparation time: 10 minutes, plus chilling
Cooking time: 6 minutes
Cals per serving: 355-290
Serves 6-8

225 g (8 oz) chicken livers	**15 ml (1 tbsp) brandy or sherry**
125 g (4 oz) streaky bacon rashers, derinded	**100 g (4 oz) butter, softened**
1 medium onion	**salt and pepper**
1 garlic clove	**TO SERVE**
10 ml (2 tsp) green peppercorns	**100 g (4 oz) butter**
15 ml (1 tbsp) wholegrain mustard	**15 ml (1 tbsp) chopped fresh parsley**

1 Trim the chicken livers and then finely chop. Finely chop the bacon. Peel and finely chop the onion. Peel and crush the garlic. Crush the green peppercorns.

2 Put the livers, bacon and onion into a large bowl with the garlic, green peppercorns, mustard and brandy.

3 Cover and cook on HIGH for 6 minutes or until the liver and bacon are tender, stirring frequently. Leave to cool.

4 Transfer to a blender or food processor. Add the softened butter and work until smooth. Season with salt and pepper to taste.

5 Press into a 600 ml (1 pint) shallow serving dish, cover and leave to cool. Chill for 2-3 hours.

6 To finish, place the butter in a medium bowl and microwave on HIGH for 1 minute. Allow to cool slightly then pour over the pâté. Sprinkle over the parsley and chill until the butter has set. Serve with hot toasted bread.

FISH AND SHELLFISH

Fish cooked in the microwave is superb. It requires minimal cooking so all the flavour, texture and moisture is retained. Care must be taken not to overcook the fish and remember it will continue to cook after it has been removed from the microwave oven. Place the thicker part of the fish towards the outer edge of the dish and, if cooking fillets, overlap the thinner tail end so the fish is of an even thickness. The fish is done when the outer edge of the flesh is opaque and it flakes easily with a fork. If it is dark and dry when removed from the cooker then the fish has been over-cooked. When cooking fish whole, slash each side two or three times depending on the size of the fish. Not only does this make the fish look more attractive but it also helps the heat to penetrate more evenly. Brush the skin of the fish with melted butter to prevent the flesh drying out and also to give the fish extra flavour.

Fish cooking smells penetrating the house are also reduced to a minimum when the microwave oven is used. If a fish smell lingers in the microwave oven itself boil some water with a little added lemon juice in the oven for a few minutes and the smell should disappear.

For detailed instruction on thawing and cooking specific fish turn to the charts on page 120.

Grey Mullet stuffed with Herbs

As the mullet cooks the distinct flavours of the hazelnuts, garlic and butter seeps into the flesh to give a tasty and succulent fish.

Preparation time: 10 minutes
Cooking time: 8-9 minutes
Cals per serving: 550-365
Serves: 2-3

50 g (2 oz) hazelnuts	**45 ml (3 tbsp) chopped fresh herbs such as parsley, basil, tarragon, chervil, mint, coriander**
1 grey mullet, weighing about 700 g (1½ lb), scaled and gutted	**salt and pepper**
3 garlic cloves	**15 ml (1 tbsp) olive oil**
finely grated rind and juice of 1 lemon	**TO GARNISH**
	fresh herbs

1 Spread out the hazelnuts on a plate and cook on HIGH for 2-3 minutes or until lightly toasted. If they still have the skins on rub the nuts a few at a time in a piece of cloth to remove them. Set aside to cool.

2 Using a sharp knife, slash the fish three or four times on each side. Peel the garlic.

3 Put the nuts, garlic, lemon rind, half the lemon juice and the herbs in a blender or food processor and work to a coarse paste. Season to taste with salt and pepper. Spoon a little of the paste into the slashes and use the rest to stuff the fish.

4 Place the fish on a large heatproof serving plate. Mix the remaining lemon juice with the oil and spoon over the fish. Season generously with pepper.

5 Cover and cook on HIGH for 6 minutes or until tender. Serve garnished with fresh herbs.

Lime Stuffed Mackerel

Grated apple and parsnip flavoured with coriander and lime are combined to make a stuffing for these fresh mackerel. To complete the dish, overlapping slices of lime are placed on top of the mackerel before cooking.

Preparation time: 20 minutes
Cooking time: 5½ minutes, plus standing
Cals per serving: 660
Serves 2

2 mackerel, each about 225-275 g (8-10 oz), gutted	**50 g (2 oz) butter**
1 small dessert apple	**15 ml (1 tbsp) chopped fresh coriander**
125 g (4 oz) parsnips	**TO SERVE**
2 limes	**cream of horseradish sauce**

1 Diagonally slash each side of the fish two or three times. Peel and grate the apple and parsnips. Grate the rind and squeeze the juice from one and a half limes. Slice the remaining half.

2 Place the butter in a small bowl and microwave on HIGH for 30 seconds, to melt. Stir in the grated apple, parsnip, lime rind and juice and coriander.

3 Divide the stuffing between the cleaned cavities of the mackerel. Place the fish in a lightly greased shallow dish.

4 Arrange the lime slices, slightly overlapping, on top of the fish. Cover with microwave food wrap. Microwave on HIGH for 5 minutes or until the flesh is firm to the touch and almost cooked. Leave to STAND for 5 minutes.

5 Serve on warmed serving plates with cream of horseradish sauce.

Sea Bass with Thai Stuffing

The aroma from the Thai stuffing is truly wonderful! The sea bass is stuffed with a spicy paste before cooking and served, topped with slices of mango.

Preparation time: 20 minutes
Cooking time: 7-8 minutes
Cals per serving: 230
Serves 4

1 sea bass, about 700 g (1½ lb), scaled and gutted	**30 ml (2 tbsp) lime juice**
2 shallots	**15 ml (1 tbsp) light soy sauce**
1 garlic clove	**30 ml (2 tbsp) olive oil**
2.5 cm (1 inch) piece fresh root ginger	**black pepper**
1 red chilli	**TO GARNISH**
45 ml (3 tbsp) chopped fresh coriander	**1 small firm mango**
1 lemon grass stalk	**fresh sprigs of coriander**

1 Wash the fish inside and out, then dry. Using a sharp knife cut 4 deep slashes in each side of the fish.

2 Make the stuffing. Peel the shallots, garlic and ginger. Cut the chilli in half and remove the seeds. Place the shallots, garlic, chilli, coriander, root ginger and lemon grass in a food processor or blender and finely chop.

3 Spread the stuffing inside the cavity and spoon a little into each of the slashes. Place the fish on a large heatproof plate, curving slightly, if necessary.

4 Mix the lime juice, soy sauce and olive oil together and sprinkle over the dish. Season generously with pepper. Cover and cook on HIGH for 7-8 minutes, or until tender.

5 Meanwhile peel and stone the mango, then slice the flesh. Transfer the fish to a warmed serving plate. Arrange the mango slices on top of the fish and scatter with coriander sprigs.

VARIATIONS

Sea bass tastes delicious in this recipe, however the stuffing is equally good with less expensive fish such as salmon, grey mullet or sea trout.

Trout with Saffron Sauce

Fresh trout fillets are marinated in olive oil, flavoured with onion, lemon and tarragon. The marinade is then used to make a sauce which is subtly flavoured and coloured with saffron.

Preparation time: 10 minutes, plus marinating
Cooking time: 6¼-7½ minutes, plus standing
Cals per serving: 210

Serves 4

1 small onion	**salt and pepper**
4 trout fillets, each about 75 g (3 oz)	**pinch saffron threads**
30 ml (2 tbsp) lemon juice	**60 ml (4 tbsp) double cream**
15 ml (1 tbsp) chopped fresh tarragon	**1 egg yolk**
15 ml (1 tbsp) olive oil	**TO GARNISH**
	fresh sprigs of tarragon

1 Peel the onion and finely slice. Arrange the trout fillets in a single layer, skin side down, in a shallow dish. Sprinkle over the lemon juice, onions, tarragon and olive oil. Season well with black pepper.

2 Cover loosely with microwave food wrap and leave to marinate for 30 minutes.

3 Microwave on HIGH for 4-5 minutes, until the flesh is firm to the touch and just cooked. Re-arrange the fish after 3 minutes.

4 Transfer the fish to a warm plate. Strain the stock into a jug and measure 90 ml (6 tbsp). Make up with water, if necessary. Add the saffron and microwave on HIGH for 1 minute. Leave to infuse for 5 minutes, stirring occasionally.

5 Meanwhile carefully remove the skin from the fish and arrange on a warm serving plate. Keep warm.

6 Add the cream to the sauce and microwave on HIGH for 1 minute. Quickly whisk in the egg yolk so the ingredients are blended. Season with salt and pepper. Microwave on MEDIUM for 15-30 seconds, or until slightly thickened. Do not over-cook or the sauce will curdle.

7 Serve the sauce spooned over the fish and garnish with sprigs of tarragon.

Rolled Plaice with Pesto

These succulent plaice rolls, flavoured with basil, pine nuts and Parmesan cheese make the perfect, quick dinner party meal. Serve on a bed of stir-fried vegetables or spaghetti.

Preparation time: 15 minutes
Cooking time: 7 minutes
Cals per serving: 145
Serves: 4

8 small plaice fillets about 650g (1 lb) total weight	**30 ml (2 tbsp) lemon juice**
15 ml (1 tbsp) green pesto	**100 ml (4 fl oz) fish or chicken stock**

1 Skin the plaice fillets and divide each one along the centre line into 2 fillets. Roll up loosely with the skinned side on the inside. Arrange in a single layer in a heatproof dish.

2 Put the pesto, lemon juice and fish or chicken stock into a jug. Microwave on HIGH for 1 minute then pour the mixture over the fish rolls.

3 Cover the dish and cook the fish on HIGH for 6 minutes until tender.

4 Serve on a bed of stir-fried vegetables or on a bed of spaghetti tossed in a tomato sauce.

Lime and Honey Poached Salmon

A lime dressing adds a special flavour to this dish of salmon steaks, served on a bed of tender-crisp courgettes and beans.

Preparation time: 10 minutes
Cooking time: 6 minutes
Cals per serving: 415
Serves: 2

125 g (4 oz) courgettes	**15 ml (1 tbsp) olive oil**
125 g (4 oz) French beans	**5 ml (1 tsp) clear honey**
30 ml (2 tbsp) chopped fresh parsley	**salt and pepper**
1 lime	**2 salmon steaks or cutlets each weighing about 175 g (6 oz)**

1 Trim the courgettes and French beans. Cut the courgettes into 7.5cm (3 inch) pieces. Cut each piece into thin sticks. Cut the French beans in half.

2 Put the courgettes and French beans into a large shallow dish and sprinkle with the parsley.

3 Grate the rind from the lime and mix with 5 ml (1 tsp) lime juice, the olive oil and honey. Season with salt and pepper to taste. Pour over the vegetables.

4 Place the salmon side by side on top of the vegetables. Cover and cook on MEDIUM for 6 minutes until the fish is tender. Serve hot with new potatoes.

Salmon and Thyme Parcels

These salmon fillets are cooked inside paper parcels. The most amazing aroma from the garlic and herbs is released when they are served.

Preparation time: 15 minutes
Cooking time: 5 minutes
Cals per serving: 375
Serves: 2

2 salmon fillets, each weighing 150 g (5 oz)	**5 ml (1 tsp) mustard seeds**
salt and pepper	**10 ml (2 tsp) chopped fresh thyme**
1 small garlic clove	**2 tomatoes**
25 g (1 oz) butter, softened	**TO GARNISH**
	thyme sprigs

1 Place the salmon fillets on squares of buttered greaseproof paper and season to taste with salt and pepper.

2 Peel and crush the garlic. Blend together the garlic, butter, mustard seeds, thyme and seasoning.

3 Skin, deseed and chop the tomatoes. Top each salmon fillet with the butter and tomatoes. Draw up the corners of the greaseproof paper and tie with string to form a bundle.

4 Place on a heatproof plate and microwave on HIGH for 5 minutes or until the salmon is just cooked.

5 Serve the fish on warmed serving plates. Untie the bundles and open the greaseproof paper. Finish with fresh thyme sprigs.

Two Way Haddock Casserole

Fresh and smoked haddock compliment each other in this appetising recipe. The haddock is mixed with an array of colourful vegetables and last but by no means least with prawns and cream, to make this dish complete.

Preparation time: 15 minutes
Cooking time: 22½-24½ minutes
Cals per serving: 400
Serves: 4

450 g (1 lb) fresh haddock fillet	30 ml (2 tbsp) plain white flour
225 g (½ lb) smoked haddock fillet	15 ml (1 tbsp) paprika pepper
225 g (8 oz) onions	300 ml (½ pint) fish or chicken stock
225 g (8 oz) potatoes	125 g (4 oz) cooked peeled prawns
175 g (6 oz) carrots	150 ml (¼ pint) single cream
225 g (8 oz) courgettes	salt and pepper
25 g (1 oz) butter or margarine	30 ml (2 tbsp) chopped fresh parsley

1 Skin both haddocks and cut the flesh into large pieces. Peel the onions, potatoes, and carrots. Thinly slice the onions and thickly slice the carrots and courgettes. Cut the potatoes into large chunks.

2 Place the butter or margarine into a large bowl and microwave on HIGH for 30 seconds until melted. Add the onions, potatoes and carrots, cover and microwave on HIGH for 7 minutes stirring twice.

3 Add the courgettes. Stir in the flour, paprika pepper and stock. Cook uncovered on HIGH for 8 minutes stirring occasionally.

4 Mix in both haddocks, cover and microwave on HIGH for 6-8 minutes until the fish is cooked, stirring two or three times.

5 Stir in the prawns and single cream and season with salt and pepper. Return the dish to the microwave, cover and heat through on HIGH for 1 minute.

6 Serve sprinkled with parsley and accompanied by creamy mashed potato or crusty white bread.

Smoked Haddock Pilaf

Dried mushrooms are soaked in white wine to add extra flavour to this delicious combination of brown rice, smoked haddock, red pepper and spring onions.

Preparation time: 15 minutes
Cooking time: About 40 minutes, plus standing
Cals per serving: 430-285
Serves 4-6

15 g (½ oz) dried wild mushrooms	**1 large red pepper**
150 ml (¼ pint) dry white wine	**1 bunch spring onions**
225 g (8 oz) long grain brown rice	**25 g (1 oz) unsalted butter**
750 ml (1¼ pints) boiling hot fish stock	**30 ml (2 tbsp) chopped fresh parsley**
1 bay leaf	**30 ml (2 tbsp) freshly grated Parmesan cheese**
black pepper	**TO GARNISH**
450 g (1 lb) smoked haddock fillet	**Parmesan cheese shavings**

1 With a sharp knife or pair of scissors cut the mushrooms in half. Put the wine in a small bowl and microwave on HIGH for 30 seconds. Add the mushrooms and leave on one side to soak.

2 Wash the rice and place it in a large heatproof bowl or dish. Pour over 600 ml (1 pint) of the fish stock, add the bay leaf and season well with pepper. Stir the ingredients together then cover the dish and cook the rice on HIGH for 20 minutes. Stir the mixture once during cooking.

3 Add the mushrooms and soaking liquid, re-cover and microwave on HIGH for 12-15 minutes, or until almost all the liquid has been absorbed and the rice is almost tender.

4 Skin the fish and cut into large chunks. Cut the pepper in half, remove the seeds and thinly slice. Trim the spring onions and coarsely chop.

5 Stir the fish chunks and pepper slices into the rice, with the remaining hot stock if required. Cover the dish and microwave on HIGH for 5 minutes.

6 Stir in the spring onions, butter, parsley and freshly grated Parmesan cheese. Leave to STAND for 10 minutes. Remove the bay leaf, check the seasoning, then serve the pilaf garnished with the Parmesan cheese shavings.

Haddock and Spinach Pie

Layers of spinach, smoked haddock and cheese sauce make this tasty family pie. For a golden top, place under the grill, just before serving, to brown.

Preparation time: 20 minutes
Cooking time: 17 minutes
Cals per serving: 430
Serves: 4

50 g (2 oz) butter or margarine	**freshly grated nutmeg**
50 g (2 oz) plain white flour	**450 g (1 lb) packet frozen leaf spinach**
450 ml (¾ pint) milk	**450 g (1 lb) smoked haddock fillet**
100 g (4 oz) Cheddar cheese	**TO SERVE**
salt and pepper	**boiled or creamed potatoes**

1 Combine butter, flour and milk together in a large bowl or jug and microwave on HIGH for 4 minutes until the sauce has thickened, whisking every minute so it is smooth.

2 Grate the cheese and stir half into the sauce. Set the remaining cheese aside. Season the sauce well with salt, pepper and nutmeg. Set aside.

3 Put the frozen spinach in a deep 20.5 cm (8 inch) round dish, cover and cook on HIGH for 5 minutes until thawed, stirring once.

4 Turn into a sieve, drain thoroughly then spread evenly over the base of the dish.

5 Remove the skin from the haddock and cut the flesh into 2.5 cm (1 inch) strips. Place in a single layer over the spinach, cover and cook on HIGH for 4 minutes or until tender and the flesh flakes easily.

6 Spoon the cheese sauce over the fish to covered it completely. Microwave on HIGH for 4 minutes, then sprinkle the remaining cheese on top.

7 Brown under a hot grill if desired. Serve with boiled or creamed potatoes.

Sweet and Sour Cod Kebabs

Cubes of cod wrapped in bacon, chunks of aubergine and onion are all coated in a mouthwatering sweet and sour marinade to make these unusual fish kebabs. Serves 6 as a starter or 2-3 for a main course with rice and salad.

Preparation time: 20 minutes, plus marinating
Cooking time: 5 minutes
Cals per serving: 260
Makes: 6

450g (1 lb) thick cod fillet	**30 ml (2 tbsp) clear honey**
12 rashers streaky bacon	**15 ml (1 tbsp) soy sauce**
1 small aubergine about 125 g (4 oz)	**15 ml (1 tbsp) tomato purée**
2 small red onions	**salt and pepper**
2 lemons or limes	**TO GARNISH**
15 ml (1 tbsp) lemon juice	**lime wedges**

1 Skin the cod and cut into into 2.5 cm (1 inch) cubes. Remove the bacon rinds and stretch the bacon rashers with the back of a knife. Cut each rasher in half. Wrap a piece of bacon around each fish cube.

2 Cut the aubergine into 12 chunks. Blanch the aubergine pieces in boiling water, drain and dry on absorbent kitchen paper. Peel the onions and cut each onion in half. Cut each half into three to give twelve pieces in total. Slice the lemons or limes.

3 Thread the fish, onions, aubergines and lemon or lime slices onto 6 wooden skewers. Place the kebabs side by side in a non-metallic dish.

4 Whisk together the lemon juice, honey, soy sauce, tomato purée and seasoning. Spoon over the kebabs.

5 Cover and leave to marinate in the refrigerator for at least 12 hours turning once.

6 Arrange the kebabs side by side on a rack over a dish and microwave on HIGH for 5 minutes, re-arranging them twice during the cooking time and brushing over any remaining marinade as required.

7 Serve immediately, garnished with lime wedges.

Cod with Prawns and Cream

A creamy prawn sauce flavoured with mustard and lemon juice envelopes the succulent cod steaks as they cook to create a simple but special meal.

Preparation time: 5 minutes
Cooking time: 12 minutes
Cals per serving: 405
Serves 4

40 g (1½ oz) butter or margarine	**125 g (4 oz) peeled prawns**
1 medium onion	**10 ml (2 tsp) lemon juice**
40 g (1½ oz) plain white flour	**salt and pepper**
300 ml (½ pint) milk	**4 cod steaks each weighing about 175 g (6 oz)**
150 ml (¼ pint) single cream	**TO GARNISH**
5 ml (1 tsp) prepared mustard	**chopped fresh parsley**

1 Put the butter in a large bowl and microwave on HIGH for 30 seconds until melted.

2 Peel and chop the onion, stir into the butter, cover and microwave on HIGH for 5 minutes, stirring occasionally until softened.

3 Stir in the flour, then gradually blend in the milk and microwave on HIGH for 2 minutes until thickened, whisking after every minute.

4 Stir in the cream, mustard, prawns and lemon juice and season well with salt and pepper.

5 Arrange the fish in a single layer in a round serving dish with the thinnest parts of the cod towards the centre.

6 Spoon over the sauce and cook on HIGH for 3 minutes per 450 g (1 lb) or until the fish is tender and flakes when tested with a fork. Garnish with chopped parsley.

Egg Noodles with Prawns

The combination of hot and aromatic sauces gives an Eastern touch to this prawn noodle recipe.
Serve with salad as a main course.

Preparation time: 5 minutes
Cooking time: 4-5 minutes
Cals per serving: 550
Serves: 4

250 g (9 oz) packet thin egg noodles	225 g (8 oz) cooked peeled prawns
1 garlic clove	125 g (4 oz) bean sprouts
45 ml (3 tbsp) hoisin sauce	3 spring onions
15 ml (1 tbsp) lemon juice	black pepper
30 ml (2 tbsp) light soy sauce	TO GARNISH:
15 ml (1 tbsp) sweet chilli sauce	lemon wedges
45 ml (3 tbsp) sesame oil	spring onion tassels
50 g (2 oz) blanched almonds	

1 Put the noodles into a large heatproof bowl and pour over enough boiling water to cover them by 2.5 cm (1 inch). Cover and cook on HIGH for 2 minutes. Leave to stand, still covered, for 5 minutes while cooking the fish. Do not strain.

2 Peel and crush the garlic. Put the garlic, hoisin sauce, lemon juice, soy sauce, chilli sauce and oil into a large bowl.

3 Add the almonds, prawns, bean sprouts and drained noodles. Cover and cook on HIGH for 2-3 minutes, stirring once, until all the ingredients are hot.

4 Chop the spring onions then stir in and season to taste with black pepper.

5 To serve, spoon the mixture onto warm serving plates and garnish each serving with a lemon wedge and spring onion tassel.

Teriyaki Scallops

Tender fresh scallops are marinated in an aromatic dressing before cooking on a succulent bed of crispy vegetables. Serve for two with saffron rice or noodles or for four as a starter.

Preparation time: 15 minutes, plus marinating
Cooking time: 10-11 minutes
Cals per serving: 295-145
Serves: 2-4

450 g (1 lb) shelled large scallops	**60 ml (4 tbsp) teriyaki sauce**
2.5 cm (1 inch) piece of fresh root ginger	**2 sticks celery**
2 large garlic cloves	**1 bunch spring onions**
2.5 ml (½ tsp) chilli powder	**175 g (6 oz) carrots**
30 ml (2 tbsp) lemon juice	**45 ml (3 tbsp) chopped fresh coriander**
salt and pepper	

1 Put the scallops in a large casserole dish. Peel the ginger and thinly slice. Peel the garlic and finely chop.

2 Mix the ginger, garlic, chilli powder, lemon juice, seasoning and teriyaki sauce together. Add to the scallops, toss together, cover and leave to marinade for 1 hour.

3 Cook on HIGH for 4-5 minutes until the scallops are opaque and tender, stirring once or twice during cooking. Remove from the bowl with a slotted spoon and set aside.

4 Trim the celery and onions and slice diagonally into thin strips. Peel the carrot and cut into thin sticks. Add the carrot and celery to the casserole, cover and microwave on HIGH for 4 minutes. Stir in the spring onions and 15 ml (1 tbsp) chopped coriander.

5 Return the scallops to the casserole dish, cover and microwave on HIGH for 2 minutes until scallops are hot but vegetables are still crunchy.

6 Serve garnished with the remaining fresh coriander.

MEAT AND POULTRY

The fast, moist cooking of a microwave oven is ideal for poultry and for most cuts of meat which generally remain more tasty and juicy.

Boned and rolled meat and poultry cook more evenly, than if a bone is left in, as the shape and thickness is consistent. Overcooking or uneven cooking, especially on large rolled roasts can be prevented by shielding ends with smooth pieces of foil, shiny side inside, for part of the cooking time. Standing time is also important for larger joints as it allows them to finish cooking. Cover the joint in foil and leave it in a warm place for 15-20 minutes before checking if it is ready.

If possible select even sized and shaped cuts. Meat for stews and casseroles should be cut to a uniform size. Chops and steaks should be of the same thickness as far as possible. If cooking joints such as chicken drumsticks, which are uneven in shape, then arrange the food with the thinnest ends pointing towards the centre and change them around during cooking to ensure the heat is evenly distributed.

For detailed instruction and timings for thawing and cooking specific meat and poultry turn to page 117.

Italian Meatballs

These beef meatballs are flavoured with onion and cheese and then cooked in a colourful tomato sauce with red and green peppers.

Preparation time: 15 minutes
Cooking time: 14 minutes
Cals per serving: 330
Serves: 4

1 small onion	**1 egg**
450 g (I lb) lean minced beef	**½ small red pepper**
25 g (1 oz) fresh white breadcrumbs	**½ small green pepper**
25 g (1 oz) grated Parmesan cheese	**400ml (14 fl oz) tomato juice**
salt and pepper	**5 ml (1 tsp) chopped fresh parsley**

1 Peel the onion and chop finely. Mix together the beef, breadcrumbs, onion, cheese, salt and pepper. Beat the egg and use to bind the meatballs together.

2 With wet hands, shape the mixture into 20 small meatballs and place them in a single layer in a large casserole dish.

3 Cover and cook on HIGH for 6 minutes turning the meatballs over halfway through the cooking time.

4 Remove the core and seeds from the peppers and finely chop the flesh. Mix together with the the tomato juice and parsley. Season to taste with salt and pepper. Pour over the meatballs.

5 Re-cover and cook on HIGH for 8 minutes or until the meatballs are cooked through. Stir the mixture halfway through the cooking time.

6 Serve with plain boiled rice or cooked spaghetti.

Chilli Con Carne

Always a popular dish, it is extremely versatile and can be served on many different occasions.
Using the microwave oven, it can be made in minutes.

Preparation time: 10 minutes
Cooking time: 19-20 minutes, plus standing
Cals per serving: 305
Serves 4

1 large onion	**2.5 ml (½ tsp) ground coriander**
1 clove garlic	**400 g (14 oz) can chopped tomatoes in tomato juice**
350 g (12 oz) lean minced beef	**440g can red kidney beans**
10 ml (2 tsp) chilli powder	**TO GARNISH**
15 ml (1 tbsp) tomato purée	**15 ml (1 tbsp) chopped fresh parsley**

1 Peel and chop the onion. Peel and crush the garlic. Put the onion and garlic in a casserole dish, cover and cook on HIGH for 5-6 minutes until the onions have soften. Stir after 3 minutes.

2 Add the minced beef and chilli powder and stir to combine. Microwave, uncovered, on HIGH for 4 minutes. Stir the mince once or twice as it cooks, breaking up the pieces of meat each time.

3 Mix in the tomato purée and coriander then stir in the can of tomatoes and juice. Cover the dish and microwave on HIGH for 8 minutes, stirring twice.

4 Wash the red kidney beans and drain. Stir into the minced beef mixture and heat them through on HIGH for 2 minutes. Leave to STAND, covered, for 5 minutes then sprinkle with parsley. Serve with crusty bread or rice and a salad.

VARIATION

Use the chilli con carne mixture as a filling for Tacos. It is sufficient for 12 shells.

Heat 6 tacos shells at a time on HIGH for 30 seconds. Place a little of the chilli con carne mixture into each shell then top with a selection of shredded lettuce, grated cheese, sliced tomatoes, soured cream and peeled and sliced avocado. Serve immediately.

Lamb and Bacon Pasta

An easy to prepare pasta dish with lamb, bacon and vegetables in a creamy garlic, herb and cheese sauce. Serve with a tomato and onion salad.

Preparation time: 10 minutes
Cooking time: 26 minutes, plus standing
Cals per serving: 710
Serves 4

225 g (8 oz) pasta shells	**60 ml (4 tbsp) sun-dried tomato paste**
45 ml (3 tbsp) vegetable oil	**125 g (4 oz) medium fat cream cheese with garlic and herbs**
1 large onion	
1 garlic clove	**30 ml (2 tbsp) freshly grated Parmesan cheese**
2 sticks celery	**salt and pepper**
225 g (8 oz) smoked streaky bacon rashers	**TO SERVE**
450 g (1 lb) lean minced lamb	**15 ml (1 tbsp) chopped fresh mint or parsley**
150 ml (¼ pint) hot lamb stock	**freshly grated Parmesan cheese**

1 Place the pasta in a large deep bowl, add 900 ml (1½ pints) of boiling water and 15 ml (1 tbsp) oil. Cover and microwave on HIGH for 12 minutes.

2 Meanwhile peel and chop the onion. Peel and crush the garlic. Trim the celery and cut into thin slices.

3 Leave the pasta to STAND for 10 minutes, then drain. Place the onion, garlic and celery in a large casserole dish with the remaining oil. Cover and microwave on HIGH for 5 minutes.

4 Remove the rind from the bacon and cut the rashers into thin strips. Add to the onion mixture with the lamb. Cover and microwave on HIGH for 5 minutes, stirring occasionally to break up the minced lamb.

5 Mix in the stock and tomato paste, cover and cook on HIGH for 4 minutes. Mix in the cooked pasta, cream cheese and Parmesan cheese. Season to taste with salt and pepper. Leave to STAND for 5 minutes.

6 Serve with the fresh herbs, sprinkled over the top. Serve extra Parmesan cheese for sprinkling on top.

Lamb and Bean Casserole

A tasty warming casserole is always a favourite on a chilly winter evening. This lamb casserole is full of flavour from the leeks, carrots, celery and thyme. It is a complete meal in one pot. Just serve with chunks of crusty bread.

Preparation time: 20 minutes
Cooking time: 59 minutes
Cals per serving: 480
Serves 4

1 medium onion	**30 ml (2 tbsp) plain white flour**
1 garlic clove	**450 ml (¾ pint) lamb stock**
15 ml (1 tbsp) vegetable oil	**225 g (8 oz) can chopped tomatoes**
175 g (6 oz) leeks	**30 ml (2 tbsp) dark soy sauce**
325 g (12 oz) carrots	**15 ml (1 tbsp) chopped fresh thyme**
1 stick celery	**salt and pepper**
700 g (1½ lb) lean boneless leg or fillet of lamb	**300 g can red kidney beans**

1 Peel and chop the onion. Peel and crush the garlic and place in a microwave casserole dish with the oil. Microwave on HIGH for 4 minutes.

2 Wash the leeks and cut into thick slices. Peel the carrots and cut into sticks. Thickly slice the celery. Add to the casserole dish, stir to combine then cover and microwave on HIGH for 2 minutes.

3 Remove any fat or gristle from the lamb, then cut into 2.5 cm (1 inch) pieces. Toss with the flour. Add to the casserole dish and stir well.

4 Add the stock, tomatoes, soy sauce, thyme and season with salt and pepper. Cover and microwave on HIGH for 5 minutes. Stir, then reduce to MEDIUM for 25 minutes. Stir, re-cover and cook on LOW for 20 minutes.

5 Drain the kidney beans and stir into the casserole. Cover and cook on HIGH for 3 minutes. Serve.

Oriental Pork Escalopes

Tender pork escalopes are marinated in a ginger, garlic, coriander and soy sauce dressing, before quickly cooking. This recipe can be prepared up to a day in advance and then just cooked a few minutes before eating.

Preparation time: 15 minutes, plus marinating
Cooking time: 7-8 minutes
Cals per serving: 160
Serves: 4

2.5 cm (1 inch) piece fresh root ginger	**4 pork escalopes, about 90 g (3½ oz) each**
2 garlic cloves	**TO GARNISH**
30 ml (2 tbsp) soy sauce	**shredded spring onions**
30 ml (2 tbsp) clear honey	**lime halves**
30 ml (2 tbsp) chopped fresh coriander	

1 Grate the ginger and crush the garlic. Mix with the soy sauce, honey and coriander.

2 Place the pork escalopes in a single layer in a round shallow microwave dish and coat with the marinade.

3 Cover and refrigerate for 30 minutes. If time allows leave to marinate for at least 4 hours, preferably overnight.

4 Cover and cook on HIGH for 3 minutes. Turn the escalopes over, reposition them, re-cover and cook on MEDIUM for a further 4-5 minutes, or until the juices run clear.

5 Serve with the marinade juices poured over. Garnish with the shredded spring onions and serve with lime halves.

Honey and Mustard Gammon

A perfect mid-week supper dish. The delicate flavours from the oranges and honey add a slightly sweet and fruity flavour to the gammon. Serve with new potatoes and a selection of fresh vegetables.

Preparation time: 5 minutes
Cooking time: 8½ minutes, plus standing
Cals per serving: 535
Serves: 2

2 gammon steaks each 225 g (8 oz) in weight	**10 ml (2 tsp) French mustard**
1 medium onion	**15 ml (1 tbsp) orange blossom honey**
25 g (1 oz) butter	**5 ml (1 tsp) dark soft brown sugar**
grated rind and juice of 1 medium orange	**TO GARNISH**
	2 slices fresh orange

1 Remove the rind from the gammon steaks and snip the fat at 1 cm (½ inch) intervals – this helps to prevent the edges of the steaks curling during cooking.

2 Peel and chop the onion. Put the butter into a large, shallow dish and melt on HIGH for 30 seconds. Stir in the onion, cover the dish and microwave on HIGH for 4 minutes until the onions are soft, stirring them once.

3 Arrange the gammon steaks on top of the onions in a single layer. Mix the orange rind, orange juice, mustard, honey and sugar together and pour over the steaks.

4 Cover the dish and microwave on HIGH for 4 minutes. As the steaks cook you may hear them spitting, it is just the intense heat on the small amount of fat around the edge, it also often happens when food is grilled.

5 Leave the dish to STAND for 2 minutes. Arrange the gammon steaks on warm serving plates, pour over the sauce and garnish with the orange slices.

Pork Fillet with Vegetables

Thin strips of vegetables and pork are cooked in a tasty soy sauce, fresh ginger and sherry sauce. Perfect served with fluffy white rice.

Preparation time: 15 minutes, plus marinating

Cooking time: 6-7 minutes

Cals per serving: 280

Serves: 4

1 cm (½ inch) piece fresh root ginger	**5 ml (1 tsp) light brown soft sugar**
1 garlic clove	**450 g (1 lb) pork fillet**
30 ml (2 tbsp) vegetable oil	**225 g (8 oz) carrots**
60 ml (4 tbsp) soy sauce	**1 green pepper**
15 ml (1 tbsp) dry sherry	**3 spring onions**
12.5 ml (2½ tsp) cornflour	**225 g (8 oz) mushrooms**

1 Peel and finely chop the ginger. Peel and crush the garlic. Stir the oil, soy sauce, sherry, cornflour, sugar, ginger and garlic together in a medium casserole.

2 Cut the pork into thin strips, add to the casserole dish and stir thoroughly to coat in the marinade. Leave to marinate for at least 30 minutes.

3 Meanwhile peel the carrots and cut into matchstick strips. Halve the pepper and remove the seeds. Cut the flesh into thin strips. Cut the spring onions into 2.5 cm (1 inch) lengths. Slice the mushrooms.

4 Stir the vegetables into the pork mixture. Cover and microwave on HIGH for 6-7 minutes, stirring occasionally until the pork is tender and the vegetables are cooked through but still firm. Serve immediately.

Warm Duck and Cranberry Salad

This unusual and lively salad combines succulent duck breast slices and cranberries with a warm red wine, brandy and balsamic vinegar dressing.

Preparation time: 10 minutes
Cooking time: 11-12 minutes
Cals per serving: 530
Serves 4

2 duck breast fillets, about 350 g (12 oz)	**15 ml (1 tbsp) balsamic vinegar**
15 ml (1 tbsp) olive oil	**salt and pepper**
150 ml (¼ pint) dry red wine	**125 g (4 oz) mangetouts**
30 ml (2 tbsp) brandy	**150 g (5 oz) Continental salad leaves**
15 ml (1 tbsp) clear honey	**30 ml (2 tbsp) French dressing**
75 g (3 oz) cranberries	

1 Heat a microwave browning dish on HIGH for 8 minutes, or according to manufacturer's instructions. Place the duck fillets on the dish, skin side down. Leave until the skin is brown, then turn the fillets over.

2 Place the dish in the microwave oven and cook the fillets on MEDIUM-HIGH for 5-6 minutes. Set aside.

3 Put the olive oil, red wine, brandy and honey in a small bowl. Microwave on HIGH for 3 minutes, until the liquid has started to reduce slightly. Add the cranberries and cook for a further 2 minutes, on HIGH so the fruit starts to soften.

4 Cut the duck fillets, at an angle, into thin slices. Add to the cranberry mix and cook on HIGH for 1 minute. Stir in the balsamic vinegar and season with salt and pepper.

5 Trim the mangetouts and toss with the salad leaves and French dressing. Arrange on a serving plate. Spoon the duck, cranberries and dressing over the top. Serve immediately.

Turkey Stroganoff

A tasty sauce made with onions, mushrooms, soured cream, mustard and paprika, coats these tender strips of turkey. Serve with noodles.

Preparation time: 10 minutes
Cooking time: 16 minutes
Cals per serving: 355
Serves 4

1 large onion	**15 ml (1 tbsp) wholegrain mustard**
225 g (8 oz) mushrooms	**10 ml (2 tsp) paprika pepper**
450 g (1 lb) turkey breast fillets	**1 egg yolk**
50 g (2 oz) butter	**salt and pepper**
150 ml (¼ pint) white wine or chicken stock	**TO GARNISH**
150 ml (¼ pint) soured cream	**fresh tarragon sprigs**
30 ml (2 tbsp) tomato purée	

1 Peel and chop the onion. Slice the mushrooms. Skin the turkey and cut into thin strips. Dice the butter and place in a large bowl.

2 Microwave the butter on HIGH for 1 minute or until melted. Stir in the onion, cover and cook on HIGH for 5 minutes or until softened, stirring once.

3 Stir in the mushrooms, turkey and wine or stock. Microwave on HIGH for 6 minutes, stirring occasionally, until the turkey is tender.

4 Mix the soured cream, tomato purée, mustard, paprika pepper and egg yolk together. Stir into the meat. Cook on MEDIUM for 4 minutes or until thickened, stirring every minute. Do not allow the mixture to boil. Season with salt and pepper to taste.

5 Transfer to a warmed serving dish and garnish with tarragon sprigs.

Chinese Chicken with Peaches

The delicious smells and flavours from the soy sauce, sherry and five spice powder give this chicken recipe an authentic Chinese feel. Serve with Chinese thread noodles to complete the meal.

Preparation time: 15 minutes
Cooking time: 13½ minutes
Cals per serving: 325
Serves: 4

25 g (1 oz) butter	**15 ml (1 tbsp) sherry**
15 ml (1 tbsp) sunflower oil	**15 ml (1 tbsp) light soy sauce**
50 g (2 oz) cashew nuts	**5 ml (1 tsp) Chinese five spice powder**
1 medium onion	**20 ml (4 tsp) cornflour**
125 g (4 oz) cup mushrooms	**150 ml (¼ pint) hot chicken stock**
1 small green pepper	**205 g can sliced peaches**
350 g (12 oz) skinless chicken breast fillets	**salt and pepper**

1 Microwave the butter and oil in a heatproof dish for 30-40 seconds, or until the butter has melted. Add the cashew nuts and brown them, uncovered, on HIGH for 3 minutes stirring often. Transfer to a plate using a slotted spoon and keep on one side for later.

2 Peel and slice the onion. Slice the mushrooms. Halve the pepper, remove the seeds and cut the flesh into strips. Cut the chicken into strips.

3 Add the onion to the heatproof dish, cover and cook on HIGH for 4 minutes until almost soft, stirring once.

4 Stir the mushrooms, pepper and chicken into the onion, cover and cook on HIGH for 3 minutes, stirring 2-3 times.

5 Stir in the sherry, soy sauce, Chinese five spice powder and cornflour then gradually blend in the stock. Return the dish to the microwave and cook, covered for HIGH for a further 3 minutes.

6 Drain the peaches and chop the slices roughly. When the cooking time is complete, stir the peaches and the cashew nuts into the mixture and season with salt and pepper. Serve with Chinese medium thread noodles.

Chicken Seville

The perfect recipe for a quick but special supper. Serve with white rice and a green salad.

Preparation time: 5 minutes
Cooking time: 12 minutes, plus standing
Cals per serving: 330
Serves: 4

grated rind and juice of 2 medium oranges	**30 ml (2 tbsp) clear honey**
25 g (1 oz) butter	**4 chicken breast fillets, about 600 g (1¼ lb)**
5 ml (1 tsp) ground coriander	**salt and pepper**
5 ml (1 tsp) curry paste	**30 ml (2 tbsp) Greek-style yogurt**

1 Put the orange rind and juice into a shallow microwave dish with the butter, cut into pieces. Stir in the coriander, curry paste and honey. Cover and microwave on HIGH for 2 minutes stirring once.

2 Slash the top of each chicken breast twice, arrange in the dish and spoon over some of the sauce.

3 Cover and microwave on HIGH for 10 minutes, basting and re-arranging the chicken twice during the cooking time .

4 Season with salt and pepper then stir in the yogurt and leave to STAND for 5 minutes, covered. Serve.

Chicken in Mustard Sauce

Tender chicken breasts are served on a bed of vegetables with a creamy mustard sauce.

Preparation time: 5 minutes
Cooking time: 14½ minutes
Cals per serving: 350
Serves : 4

4 skinless chicken breast fillets	**125 g (4 oz) chestnut mushrooms**
20 ml (4 tsp) wholegrain mustard	**25 g (1 oz) butter**
15 ml (1 tbsp) vegetable oil	**150 ml (¼ pint) single cream**
1 garlic clove	**10 ml (2 tsp) Dijon mustard**
175 g (6 oz) leeks	**salt and pepper**
	30 ml (2 tbsp) chopped fresh parsley

1 Slash the chicken twice on one side, then spread on both sides with the wholegrain mustard. Arrange in a single layer in a shallow dish. Sprinkle over the the oil.

2 Peel and crush the garlic. Thickly slice the leeks and mushrooms. Place the butter in a shallow casserole dish and microwave on HIGH for 30 seconds, or until melted. Stir in the garlic, leeks and mushrooms. Cook on HIGH for 5 minutes, or until tender, stirring once.

3 Cook the chicken on HIGH for 7 minutes or until tender and the juices run clear. Re-position the chicken once during the cooking.

4 Stir the cream, mustard and 30 ml (2 tbsp) of the meat cooking juices into the vegetables and cook on HIGH for 2 minutes, stirring twice. Season with salt and pepper. Serve with the chicken, sprinkled with chopped parsley.

Chicken Risotto

Succulent pieces of chicken are cooked with mushrooms, green pepper and rice to make this simple but tasty dish. Serve with a green salad.

Preparation time: 10 minutes
Cooking time: 24-26 minutes, plus standing
Cals per serving: 630-420
Serves: 4-6

2 chicken leg portions about 450 g (1 lb)	**450 g (1 lb) long grain white rice**
30 ml (2 tbsp) corn oil	**900 ml (1½ pints) boiling chicken stock**
1 large onion	**salt and pepper**
125 g (4 oz) mushrooms	**30 ml (2 tbsp) chopped fresh parsley**
1 green pepper	

1 Cut each chicken portion into two through the joint. Pour the oil into a large casserole dish and arrange the joints in the base with the thinnest part of each portion pointing towards the centre. Cover.

2 Cook on HIGH for 6-8 minutes or until cooked turning them over halfway through the cooking. Remove from the dish and set aside to cool. Peel and chop the onion. Slice the mushrooms. Remove the core and seeds from the green pepper and slice.

3 Stir the onion, mushrooms and pepper into the remaining oil in the dish, cover and cook on HIGH for 6 minutes or until softened, stirring once.

4 Cut the chicken meat into bite-sized pieces, discarding the skin and bones and add to the casserole with the rice and stock. Mix well, cover and cook on HIGH for 12 minutes.

5 Leave to STAND, covered, for 10 minutes. Mix lightly with a fork, season with salt and pepper, stir in the chopped parsley and serve.

Chicken and Tarragon Casserole

A classic blend of chicken and tarragon come together to create this delicious casserole.
Fromage frais may be added to the sauce in place of cream for a healthier alternative.

Preparation time: 20 minutes
Cooking time: 18½ minutes, plus standing
Cals per serving: 380
Serves 4-6

1.1 kg (2½ lb) chicken	**30 ml (2 tbsp) chopped fresh tarragon**
25 g (1 oz) butter	**45 ml (3 tbsp) double cream**
1 medium onion	**salt and pepper**
½ lemon	**TO GARNISH**
15 ml (1 tbsp) plain white flour	**fresh tarragon sprigs**
300 ml (½ pint) hot chicken stock	**lemon slices**

1 Cut the chicken into joints and remove the skin. Put the butter into a large heatproof dish and microwave on HIGH for 30 seconds, or until melted. Add the chicken joints preferably in one layer, cover and microwave on HIGH for 5 minutes turning the joints over halfway through the cooking time. Transfer to a plate.

2 Peel and chop the onion. Stir into the juices in the dish, cover and microwave on HIGH for 5 minutes stirring once. Grate the rind and squeeze the juice from the lemon half.

3 Stir the flour into the casserole dish, then gradually add the hot stock, lemon rind and juice and tarragon.

4 Return the chicken to the dish, spoon over the sauce, then cover the dish and microwave the casserole on HIGH for 8 minutes, moving the joints about several times during the cooking time.

5 Stir in the cream and season well with salt and pepper. Cover the dish and leave the casserole to STAND for 10 minutes. Serve garnished with fresh tarragon and lemon slices.

VEGETABLES AND VEGETABLE ACCOMPANIMENTS

One of the best things a microwave does is to cook vegetables. Fresh vegetables cook quickly in the minimum of water so the texture, flavour, colour and nutritional flavour are retained. A microwave oven also allows you to cook single servings of vegetables with the minimum of effort.

For the best results remember to prepare vegetables so they are an even size. Irregular shaped vegetables such as broccoli spears and cauliflower florets should be arranged so the thickest parts are nearest the edge of the dish. Stir or move the vegetables at least once during cooking to ensure they cook evenly and only season them after they are cooked otherwise salt sprinkled over the surface of the food could cause dark spots.

Vegetables cooked whole such as potatoes and beetroot should be pricked several times to allow the steam to escape and prevent them from bursting as they cook. Most vegetables should be cooked covered; microwave food wrap, with a small hole left for the steam to escape is recommended or a lidded casserole dish or microwave cookware can be used. For detailed instruction and timings for cooking frozen and fresh vegetables turn to page 123.

Pasta with Asparagus

Asparagus is a wonderful vegetable and so easy to cook in the microwave oven. Combined in this simple cream and wine sauce with Parmesan cheese, it makes a prefect pasta dish.

Preparation time: 10 minutes
Cooking time: 25 minutes
Cals per serving: 845
Serves 4

200g (7 oz) extra fine asparagus	**350 g (12 oz) dried penne**
1 medium onion	**15 ml (1 tbsp) olive oil**
25 g (1 oz) butter	**75 g (3 oz) Parmesan cheese**
90 ml (3 fl oz) dry white wine	**salt and pepper**
300 ml (½ pint) double cream	

1 Trim the asparagus. Cut in half into about 5 cm (2 inch) lengths. Peel and finely chop the onion.

2 Place the asparagus spears in a medium sized casserole dish. Add 150ml (¼ pint) water, cover and cook on HIGH for 5 minutes, or until just tender. Drain.

3 Place the butter and onion in a large casserole dish, cover and cook on HIGH for 5 minutes, stirring twice. Stir in the asparagus, wine and cream. Re-cover.

4 Place the pasta in a large bowl, add 1.7 litres (3 pints) boiling water and oil. Cover with pierced microwave food wrap. Cook on HIGH for 12 minutes. Leave to STAND for 5 minutes.

5 Meanwhile, heat the sauce on HIGH for 2 minutes. Grate the Parmesan and stir half into the sauce. Season with salt and pepper. Cover and cook on HIGH for 1 minute, or until bubbling.

6 Drain the pasta and add to the sauce. Toss well to mix. Serve sprinkled with the remaining Parmesan.

Vegetable Lasagne

A spinach, mushroom and onion pasta dish, finished with an interesting cheese, crème fraîche and mustard topping. If wished, place under a grill for a golden finish.

Preparation time: 30 minutes
Cooking time: 27½ minutes, plus standing
Cals per serving: 480
Serves 4

100 g (4 oz) lasagne sheets	**450 g (1 lb) frozen chopped leaf spinach, thawed and drained thoroughly**
salt and pepper	**50 g (2 oz) Cheddar cheese**
1 large onion	**200 ml (7 fl oz) crème fraîche**
225 g (8 oz) cup mushrooms	**pinch of cayenne pepper**
1 garlic clove	**2.5 ml (½ tsp) made French mustard**
50 g (2 oz) butter	**15 ml (1 tbsp) freshly grated Parmesan cheese**

1 Pour 1.1 litres (2 pints) boiling water into a large heatproof dish. Add the lasagne sheets one by one. Cook the pasta uncovered on HIGH for 10 minutes stirring it often so the sheets remain separate. Sprinkle with salt then leave the pasta, still in the water to one side.

2 Peel and chop the onion. Quarter the mushrooms. Peel and crush the garlic. Place the butter in a large heatproof bowl and microwave on HIGH for 30-40 seconds to melt. Add the onion, mushrooms and garlic and stir to combine. Cover and cook on HIGH for 4 minutes, stirring once.

3 Stir in the drained spinach then re-cover and cook on HIGH for 3 minutes stirring it once.

4 Turn half the vegetable mixture into the base of a 1.1-1.7 litre (2-3 pint) shallow heatproof dish. Drain the lasagne and arrange half the sheets on top.

5 Repeat these layers once more so all the mixture is used. Grate the Cheddar cheese.

6 Mix the crème fraîche with the Cheddar cheese, cayenne, mustard and a little seasoning. Spread it over the top of the lasagne. Scatter the Parmesan cheese on the top.

7 Microwave on MEDIUM for 10 minutes then leave to STAND for 5 minutes before serving.

Bean Goulash

A warming casserole of dried beans combined with yellow pepper, tomatoes and mushrooms and flavoured with caraway seeds. Perfect for a vegetarian meal, served with rice or crusty bread.

Preparation time: 10 minutes, plus soaking
Cooking time: 45 minutes, plus standing
Cals per serving: 225-150
Serves 4-6

100 g (4 oz) black-eye beans	**175 g (6 oz) mushrooms**
100 g (4 oz) aduki beans	**400 g (14 oz) can chopped tomatoes**
1 yellow pepper	**90 ml (6 tbsp) natural yogurt**
1 garlic clove	**salt and pepper**
10 ml (2 tsp) caraway seeds	**TO GARNISH**
15 ml (1 tbsp) vegetable oil	**chopped fresh parsley**
15 ml (1 tbsp) paprika pepper	

1 Soak the black-eye and aduki beans overnight in plenty of cold water.

2 Drain the beans and place them in a large bowl. Pour over enough boiling water to cover by about 2.5 cm (1 inch). Cover and cook on HIGH for 35 minutes or until tender, stirring occasionally. Leave to STAND, still covered for 5 minutes. Do not drain.

3 Meanwhile cut the pepper in half, remove the seeds and coarsely chop. Peel the garlic and crush. Lightly crush the caraway seeds. Place the oil, pepper, garlic, caraway seeds and paprika pepper in a large heatproof bowl. Cover and cook on HIGH for 2 minutes stirring once.

4 Drain the beans and rinse with boiling water. Thickly slice the mushrooms. Add the beans and mushrooms to the pepper mixture with the tomatoes and their juice. Stir thoroughly, re-cover and cook on HIGH for 8 minutes stirring once.

5 Stir in 30 ml (2 tbsp) of the yogurt and season to taste with salt and pepper. Drizzle the remaining yogurt over the top and sprinkle with the parsley. Serve hot with brown rice or crusty bread.

Bulgar Wheat with Vegetables

Bulgar wheat forms the unusual base for this colourful vegetable dish with carrots, mushrooms and mangetouts. Serve as a vegetarian dish for two or as a vegetable accompaniment for four.

Preparation time: 15 minutes
Cooking time: 16-17 minutes
Cals per serving: 325
Serves: 4

1 medium onion	**125 g (4 oz) mangetouts**
1 garlic clove	**30 ml (2 tbsp) chopped fresh coriander**
15 ml (1 tbsp) vegetable oil	**75 ml (5 tbsp) natural yogurt**
1 eating apple	**25 g (1 oz) cashew nuts**
2 large carrots	**salt and pepper**
125 g (4 oz) flat mushrooms	**TO GARNISH**
225 g (8 oz) bulgar wheat	**chopped fresh coriander**

1 Peel and chop the onion. Peel and crush the garlic. Put the oil, onion and garlic into a large bowl. Cover and cook on HIGH for 5 minutes or until softened, stirring once.

2 Peel and coarsely grate the apple and carrots. Roughly chop the mushrooms. Stir in the bulgar wheat, apple, carrots, mushrooms and 150 ml (¼ pint) boiling water. Cover and cook on HIGH for 10 minutes or until softened, stirring occasionally.

3 Trim the mangetouts and cut in half. Stir into the bulgar mixture and cook on HIGH for 1-2 minutes or until just tender.

4 Mix the coriander and yogurt together. Coarsely chop the cashew nuts. Stir into the wheat mixture with the yogurt mixture. Season to taste with salt and pepper. Mix thoroughly to combine.

5 Transfer to a warmed serving dish, sprinkle with coriander and serve.

Vegetable Korma

A mild vegetable curry dish. Carrots, cauliflower, parsnips, potatoes and courgettes are used in this recipe, but chop and change to include your own favourites.

Preparation time: 20 minutes
Cooking time: 22-24 minutes
Cals per serving: 520-345
Serves: 4-6

1 large onion	**10 ml (2 tsp) turmeric**
2.5 cm (1 inch) piece fresh root ginger	**finely grated rind and juice of ½ lime or lemon**
1-2 garlic cloves	**50 g (2 oz) ground almonds**
15 ml (1 tbsp) vegetable oil	**200 ml (7 fl oz) double cream**
15 ml (1 tbsp) coriander seeds	**salt**
5 ml (1 tsp) whole cloves	**TO GARNISH**
6 green cardamom pods (seeds only)	**50 g (2 oz) flaked almonds, toasted**
10 ml (2 tsp) black peppercorns	**45 ml (3 tbsp) chopped fresh coriander**
900 g (2 lbs) mixed vegetables including carrots, potatoes, parsnips, cauliflower and courgettes	

1 Peel and finely chop the onion and ginger. Peel and crush the garlic. Place the oil in a large casserole dish and microwave on HIGH for 30 seconds.

2 Add the onion, ginger and garlic, cover and microwave on HIGH for 5-7 minutes until starting to soften, stirring once.

3 Grind the coriander seeds, cloves, cardamom seeds and peppercorns in an electric grinder or using a pestle and mortar. Add to the casserole dish, stir well then re-cover and microwave on HIGH for 1 minute.

4 Peel the carrots, potatoes and parsnips. Cut into chunks. Break the cauliflower into small florets. Cut the courgettes into chunks.

5 Add all the vegetables to the dish, with the turmeric, lime or lemon rind and juice, the ground almonds and 150 ml (¼ pint) boiling water. Stir well, cover and microwave on HIGH for 15 minutes, or until the vegetables are cooked, stirring twice.

6 Carefully stir in the cream. Season with salt to taste. Sprinkle with the toasted flaked almonds (see page 13) and coriander and serve.

Tomato and Parsnip Layer

Thinly sliced parsnips are cooked with onions and garlic, before mixing with a cheese and basil.
To make the layers the parsnips are interleaved with tomato slices.

Preparation time: 20 minutes
Cooking time: 12 minutes, plus standing
Cals per serving: 205
Serves: 4

450 g (1 lb) tomatoes	**40g (1½ oz) fresh brown breadcrumbs**
1 medium onion	**30 ml (2 tbsp) grated Parmesan cheese**
225 g (8 oz) parsnips	**15 ml (1 tbsp) chopped fresh basil**
1 garlic clove	**25g packet ready salted crisps**
15 ml (1 tbsp) oil	

1 Skin and slice the tomatoes. Peel and chop the onion. Peel and thinly slice the parsnips. Peel and crush the garlic. Put the onion, parsnips, garlic and oil into a bowl, cover and microwave on HIGH for 4 minutes stirring once.

2 Mix in the breadcrumbs, cheese and basil. Arrange half the tomatoes in a layer in the bottom of a 1.1 litre (2 pint) heatproof dish.

3 Arrange half the parsnip mixture on top. Repeat these two layers then cover the dish and microwave on HIGH for 8 minutes until the vegetables are almost soft.

4 Leave the dish to STAND for 5 minutes then sprinkle the crushed crisps over the surface and serve at once.

Spicy Cauliflower with Yogurt

A spicy vegetable dish made with cauliflower, onion, apple and peas tossed in natural yogurt and fresh coriander.

Preparation time: 10 minutes
Cooking time: 16-18 minutes
Cals per serving: 175-115
Serves: 4-6

1 medium onion	**1 small cooking apple**
30 ml (2 tbsp) vegetable oil	**125 g (4 oz) frozen peas**
5 ml (1 tsp) medium curry powder	**150 ml (¼ pint) natural yogurt**
2.5 ml (½ tsp) mustard powder	**10 ml (2 tsp) cornflour**
2.5 ml (½ tsp) turmeric	**salt and pepper**
pinch of cayenne pepper	**TO GARNISH**
1 large cauliflower	**chopped fresh coriander**

1 Peel and chop the onion. Put the oil, curry powder, mustard, turmeric, cayenne pepper and onion in a large bowl, cover and microwave on HIGH for 5-7 minutes, until the onion has softened, stirring occasionally.

2 Trim the cauliflower and break into small florets. Peel, core and chop the apple. Add the cauliflower and apple to the onion mixture.

3 Cover and microwave on HIGH for 10 minutes, stirring occasionally until just tender. Stir in the peas.

4 Blend the yogurt into the cornflour then stir it into the cauliflower mixture.

5 Microwave on HIGH for 1 minute until heated through. Season well with salt and pepper. Transfer to a warmed serving dish, sprinkle with chopped coriander and serve.

Potato and Parsley Bake

A tasty dish of thinly sliced potatoes cooked with onion, garlic and soured cream.
It is served sprinkled with cheese. Finish under a grill for a golden brown top. Serve as an
accompaniment to meat and fish dishes.

Preparation time: 15 minutes
Cooking time: 21½-22½ minutes
Cals per serving: 320
Serves: 4

1 medium onion	**30 ml (2 tbsp) milk**
1 garlic clove	**45 ml (3 tbsp) chopped fresh parsley**
25 g (1 oz) butter	**salt and pepper**
700 g (1½ lb) potatoes	**50 g (2 oz) Cheddar cheese**
150 ml (¼ pint) soured cream	**TO GARNISH**
	chopped fresh parsley

1 Peel and thinly slice the onion. Peel and crush the garlic. Put the butter in a shallow dish and microwave on HIGH for 30 seconds or until melted.

2 Stir in the onion and garlic, cover and microwave on HIGH for 5 minutes or until the onion has softened, stirring once.

3 Peel the potatoes and very thinly slice. Add the potatoes, cream, milk and parsley to the dish. Season with salt and pepper then carefully mix together so the potato slices are coated with the cream mixture.

4 Re-cover and microwave on HIGH for 15 minutes or until the potatoes are cooked.

5 Grate the cheese and sprinkle over the potatoes. Microwave on HIGH for 1-2 minutes until the cheese has melted.

6 Brown under a hot grill, if desired. Serve garnished with chopped parsley.

Pepper, Okra and Onion Medley

A colourful combination of vegetables with an interesting taste and texture. Ideal for serving as an accompaniment to a roast meal.

Preparation time: 10 minutes
Cooking time: 9½-10½ minutes, plus standing
Cals per serving: 150
Serves: 4

225 g (8 oz) onions	**125 g (4 oz) okra**
50 g (2 oz) butter	**15 ml (1 tbsp) chopped fresh marjoram**
1 red pepper	**salt and pepper**
1 green pepper	

1 Peel and slice the onions. Put the butter into a heatproof dish and microwave on HIGH for 30-40 seconds until melted. Stir in the onions, cover the dish and microwave on HIGH for 3 minutes, stirring once.

2 Cut the peppers in half, remove the core and seeds and slice the flesh into strips.

3 Trim the okra, cut into 5 cm (2 inch) pieces and stir into the dish with the peppers and marjoram so they are coated with the melted butter.

4 Re-cover the dish and cook on HIGH for 6-7 minutes stirring twice. Season with salt and pepper, to taste. Leave to STAND for 2 minutes before serving.

Buttered Carrots

A tasty dressing of butter, onion, sugar and parsley, turns this every day vegetable into a dish to remember.

Preparation time: 10 minutes
Cooking time: 10-12 minutes, plus standing
Cals per serving: 85
Serves: 4

1 small onion	**30 ml (2 tbsp) water**
450 g (1 lb) carrots	**salt**
15 g (½ oz) butter	**15 ml (1 tbsp) chopped fresh parsley**
15 ml (1 tbsp) demerara sugar	

1 Peel and chop the onion. Peel and thinly slice the carrots. Put the butter, onion, carrots, sugar and water into a shallow casserole dish, cover and cook on HIGH for 10-12 minutes, stirring once.

2 Season with salt, to taste. Sprinkle over the parsley then leave the vegetables, to STAND, covered, for 3 minutes to finish cooking before serving.

Ratatouille

This classic but simple to prepare vegetable dish cooks excellently in the microwave oven as all the fresh Mediterranean vegetables stay bright and colourful.

Preparation time: 20 minutes
Cooking time: 21 minutes, plus standing
Cals per serving: 140
Serves: 4

1 medium aubergine	**350 g (12 oz) onions**
salt and pepper	**1 large garlic clove**
1 red pepper	**30 ml (2 tbsp) olive oil**
450 g (1 lb) fresh tomatoes	**pinch of sugar**
450 g (1 lb) courgettes	**1 bay leaf**

1 Trim the aubergine and cut into small pieces then place in a colander over a plate. Sprinkle with salt and leave it on one side for 20 minutes so the salt can draw out the excess moisture. Rinse, drain and pat dry.

2 Cut the pepper in half, remove the core and seeds and cut the flesh into strips. Skin the tomatoes and cut into quarters. Trim and slice the courgettes. Peel and slice the onions. Peel and crush the garlic.

3 Put the oil into a large heatproof dish and microwave on HIGH for 1 minute. Stir in the aubergines, tomatoes, courgettes, pepper, onion and garlic. Sprinkle over the sugar and nestle the bay leaf into the mixture.

4 Cover the dish and microwave on HIGH for 20 minutes, stirring it several times during the cooking

5 Finally add plenty of seasoning then leave the dish to STAND for 10 minutes so the vegetables are completely soft.

6 Remove the bay leaf and serve either hot as a vegetable accompaniment or chill and serve sprinkled with grated Parmesan cheese either as a first course or salad.

Red Cabbage with Caraway

A tasty vegetable dish of red cabbage cooked with caraway seeds, nutmeg, onion, garlic, apple and redcurrant jelly.

Preparation time: 15 minutes
Cooking time: 18 minutes, plus standing
Cals per serving: 95
Serves: 4

700 g (1½ lb) red cabbage	**a pinch of freshly grated nutmeg**
1 large onion	**30 ml (2 tbsp) redcurrant jelly**
1 garlic clove	**225 g (8 oz) cooking apples**
60 ml (4 tbsp) red wine vinegar	**salt and pepper**
2.5 ml (½ tsp) caraway seeds	

1 Trim the cabbage and shred it finely. Peel and slice the onion. Peel and crush the garlic.

2 Put the vinegar, caraway seeds, nutmeg and redcurrant jelly into a large casserole dish. Stir in 60 ml (4 tbsp) cold water. Cover and microwave on HIGH for 3 minutes, stirring once.

3 Stir in the cabbage, onion and garlic, cover the dish and cook on HIGH for 10 minutes, stirring once.

4 Peel and chop the apples. Stir into the cabbage mixture. Cover and microwave on HIGH for a further 5 minutes until the mixture is tender and well blended.

5 Check the vegetable dish for seasoning then leave to STAND for 5 minutes before serving.

SNACKS

The microwave oven is ideal for snacks. It is perfect when you want a meal that can be quickly and easily cooked.

Jacket potatoes cooked in the microwave take less than a quarter of the conventional time if baked in the oven. They can be served either topped with butter and perhaps grated cheese or filled with one of the tasty fillings suggested in this chapter.

Eggs are another very popular snack meal and there are a host of ways in which they can be cooked in the microwave. However never attempt to microwave an egg in its shell as it will explode. Also remember the white and yolk of an egg cook at different speeds so when poaching or baking slightly undercook and allow a standing time so the process is completed evenly.

Smoked Salmon Scramble

Serve this lightly scrambled egg, and smoked salmon, with triangles of hot toasted bread.

Preparation time: 10 minutes
Cooking time: 3½-4 minutes
Cals per serving: 420
Serves 2

4 eggs	**25 g (1 oz) butter**
45 ml (3 tbsp) crème fraîche	**75 g (3 oz) smoked salmon**
salt and pepper	**TO GARNISH**
paprika	**30 ml (2 tbsp) snipped chives**

1 Whisk together the eggs, crème fraîche, 30 ml (2 tbsp) cold water, salt, pepper and a pinch of paprika.

2 Place the butter in a medium bowl and cook on HIGH for 30 seconds, or until melted. Add the egg mixture and stir into the melted fat.

3 Cook on HIGH for 2½-3 minutes, or until the eggs are just beginning to set, stirring frequently.

4 Cut the smoked salmon into thin strips and stir into the egg mixture. Cook on HIGH for 30 seconds, or until eggs are lightly scrambled. Stir to scramble. Sprinkle with snipped chives and serve immediately.

Moules Marinières

This is a perfect dish for the microwave oven. The mussels are quickly poached with white wine, garlic and onion to make a succulent dish. The sauce is enriched with cream just before serving.

Preparation time: 5 minutes
Cooking time: 7-8 minutes
Cals per serving: 615
Serves: 2

900 g (2 lb) fresh mussels	**25 g (1 oz) butter**
1 small onion	**150 ml (¼ pint) double cream**
1 garlic clove	**pinch saffron strands**
150 ml (¼ pint) dry white wine	**salt and pepper**
15 ml (1 tbsp) chopped fresh parsley	**45 ml (3 tbsp) chopped fresh parsley**

1 Clean the mussels. Peel and finely chop the onion. Peel and crush the garlic. Put the onion, garlic, wine, parsley and 45 ml (3 tbsp) water into a large bowl and cook on HIGH for 2 minutes.

2 Stir in the mussels, cover and cook on HIGH for 4 minutes or until all the mussels have opened, removing the mussels on the top as they open and shaking the bowl occasionally. Discard any mussels which do not open.

3 Strain the mussels through a sieve and return the cooking liquid to the bowl. Put the mussels into two warm, large soup bowls.

4 Stir the butter, cream and saffron into the cooking liquid. Cook on HIGH for 1-2 minutes or until hot, stirring often. Season with salt and pepper to taste.

5 Pour the sauce over the mussels. Sprinkle with plenty of chopped parsley and serve immediately with French bread to mop up the juices.

Soused Herrings

These freshly prepared herrings are poached in a spiced cider vinegar.

Preparation time: 15 minutes
Cooking time: 6 minutes
Cals per serving: 225
Serves 4

4 fresh herrings	**2 small bay leaves**
salt and pepper	**6 juniper berries**
150 ml (¼ pint) cider vinegar	**4 whole cloves**
3-4 black peppercorns	**1 small onion**

1 Clean and bone the herrings. Trim the heads, tails and fins from the fish. Remove any remaining bones. A pair of tweezers is the best tool for this job. Sprinkle the inside of the fish with salt and pepper.

2 Roll the fish up, skin side out, starting at the head end and secure with wooden cocktail sticks. Arrange in a single layer in a shallow dish.

3 Mix the vinegar with 150 ml (¼ pint) water, add the peppercorns, bay leaves, juniper berries and cloves and pour the liquid over the fish. Peel and slice the onion. Arrange the slices on top of the fish.

4 Cover and microwave on HIGH for 6 minutes turning the fish over after 3 minutes. Cool in the liquid, then chill and serve with a salad.

French Bread Pizza

The perfect snack when food is needed in a hurry. These french bread halves are topped with tomato, onion, garlic and herbs, then sprinkled with cheese which melts on cooking.

Preparation time: 10 minutes
Cooking time: 6-8 minutes
Cals per serving: 575
Serves: 2

15 ml (1 tbsp) vegetable oil	**1 small French loaf**
1 small onion	**60 ml (4 tbsp) sun-dried tomato paste or pesto**
1 garlic clove	**25 g (1 oz) mozzarella cheese**
400 g (14 oz) can chopped tomatoes	**75 g (3 oz) Cheddar cheese**
15 ml (1 tbsp) tomato purée	**few black olives**
5 ml (1 tsp) dried mixed herbs	**anchovy fillets (optional)**
salt and pepper	

1 Put the vegetable oil in a medium sized bowl. Peel the onion and chop. Peel the garlic and crush. Drain the tomatoes. Place the onion, garlic, tomatoes, tomato purée, herbs and salt and pepper in the bowl. Microwave, uncovered, on HIGH for 5-7 minutes or until thoroughly hot and slightly reduced.

2 Cut the French bread in half horizontally then cut each length in half. Place crust side down, side by side, on a large flat serving plate. Spread each slice with 15 ml (1 tbsp) of sun-dried tomato paste or pesto.

3 Spoon the tomato topping onto the bread. Grate the mozzarella and Cheddar cheeses. Sprinkle over the tomato topping. Arrange the olives and anchovies, if using, on top of the cheese.

4 Microwave on HIGH for 1-2 minutes until heated through and the cheese has started to melt. Serve immediately.

Spaghetti Carbonara

This popular dish is excellent made in the microwave oven. Tender strands of spaghetti are coated in a creamy egg, bacon and cheese sauce.

Preparation time: 5 minutes
Cooking time: 14 minutes
Cals per serving: 890-670
Serves: 3-4

225 g (8 oz) spaghetti	**45 ml (3 tbsp) freshly grated Parmesan cheese**
salt and pepper	**150 ml (¼ pint) double cream**
225 g (8 oz) streaky bacon rashers	**TO GARNISH**
2 eggs	**chopped fresh parsley**
125 g (4 oz) Cheddar cheese	**freshly grated Parmesan cheese**

1 Put the spaghetti and salt to taste into a large bowl. Pour over enough boiling water to cover by about 2.5 cm (1 inch). Stir, then cover and cook on HIGH for 8 minutes or until almost tender, stirring twice. Leave to stand, covered for 5 minutes while making the sauce. Do not drain.

2 Remove the rind from the bacon. Chop the rashers and place in a medium bowl, cover with absorbent kitchen paper, and microwave on HIGH for 5 minutes until slightly crisp.

3 Lightly beat the eggs. Grate the Cheddar cheese. and beat into the eggs with the Parmesan cheese. Stir the cream into the bacon and season with salt and pepper. Microwave on HIGH for 1 minute until heated through.

4 Drain the spaghetti well and pour over the egg and cheese mixture. Mix well, then stir in the bacon and cream mixture so all the ingredients are well blended.

5 Transfer to warmed serving plates. Sprinkle with parsley and Parmesan and serve at once.

Cheese and Salami Pie

This is an ideal tasty snack for one. Thinly sliced potatoes are cooked with onions and salami and topped with a cheesy breadcrumb coating.

Preparation time: 10 minutes
Cooking time: 6 minutes, plus standing
Cals per serving: 595
Serves: 1

125 g (4 oz) potatoes	**freshly grated nutmeg**
½ small onion	**50 g (2 oz) Gruyère cheese**
25 g (1 oz) thinly sliced salami	**30 ml (2 tbsp) fresh breadcrumbs**
salt and pepper	**10 ml (2 tsp) grated Parmesan cheese**

1 Peel and thinly slice the potatoes and onion. Cut the salami into thin strips. Layer the sliced potatoes into an individual round dish with the onion and salami. Season with salt, pepper and nutmeg.

2 Cover and cook on HIGH for 4 minutes or until the potatoes are almost tender.

3 Grate the Gruyère cheese and mix with the breadcrumbs and Parmesan. Uncover the potatoes and sprinkle the cheese mixture evenly over the top.

4 Cook on HIGH for 2 minutes. Leave to STAND for 5 minutes then serve with a green salad.

Cheese Fondue

A perfect recipe for casual entertaining. By cooking the fondue in the microwave oven any fear of the mixture burning and sticking to the dish, is eliminated.

Preparation time: 10 minutes
Cooking time: 9-11 minutes
Cals per serving: 645
Serves: 4

1 garlic clove	**15 ml (1 tbsp) gin**
300 ml (½ pint) dry white wine	**pinch of nutmeg**
5 ml (1 tsp) lemon juice	**TO SERVE**
350 g (12 oz) Gouda cheese	**French bread, cut into small pieces**
225 g (8 oz) Gruyère cheese	**cherry tomatoes**
30 ml (2 tbsp) cornflour	**pieces of green pepper**

1 Peel the garlic and cut in half. Place it in a heatproof dish with the white wine and lemon juice. Cover and microwave on HIGH for 4 minutes, or until the wine boils.

2 Meanwhile grate the Gouda and Cheddar cheeses. Remove the dish from the microwave and gradually stir in the cheese, so it starts to melt.

3 Blend the cornflour with the gin and a little water to make a smooth paste. Stir it into the cheese mixture and add a pinch of nutmeg.

4 Cover the dish and microwave on MEDIUM for 3 minutes. Beat thoroughly and return to the microwave oven.

5 Cook on MEDIUM for 2-4 minutes or until the fondue thickens. Beat thoroughly using a balloon whisk, until smooth. It is ready when it resembles a very thick cheese sauce. Be careful not to overcook the ingredients as the cheese could become rubbery. Remove the garlic pieces.

6 Carefully transfer the fondue to a china fondue dish and place it on the table over a lighted spirit stove so the mixture remains warm.

7 Serve with a basket of French bread pieces, cherry tomatoes and pieces of green pepper for your guests to skewer and dip into the hot fondue.

Macaroni Cheese

Both young and old adore this family dish. Tender pieces of pasta are coated in a cheesy sauce, flavoured with chives.

Preparation time: 5 minutes
Cooking time: 17 minutes, plus standing
Cals per serving: 575
Serves: 4

175 g (6 oz) short cut macaroni	**600 ml (1 pint) milk**
10 ml (2 tsp) sunflower oil	**225 g (8 oz) mature Cheddar cheese**
salt and pepper	**15 ml (1 tbsp) wholegrain mustard**
25 g (1 oz) butter	**30 ml (2 tbsp) chopped fresh chives**
25 g (1 oz) plain white flour	

1 Put the macaroni and oil into a very large heatproof bowl. Pour over sufficient boiling water to cover the pasta by 2.5 cm (1 inch). Stir, then cover the bowl with microwave food wrap, leaving a small air gap. Microwave on HIGH for 10 minutes stirring twice.

2 Add a little salt, then leave the pasta, still covered, for 5 minutes to complete the cooking.

3 Meanwhile cut the butter into small pieces. Place the butter, flour and milk into a large jug and blend well together. Microwave the sauce on HIGH for 5 minutes, uncovered, until it has boiled and thickened, whisking after every minute.

4 Grate the cheese and reserve 30 ml (2 tbsp). Stir the remainder into the sauce with the mustard and chives. Season well with salt and pepper.

5 Drain the macaroni, return it to the bowl and stir in the sauce. Cover and heat the ingredients together on HIGH for 2 minutes, stirring once.

6 Transfer the macaroni cheese into a warmed serving dish. Sprinkle with the reserved grated cheese and place under a preheated grill to brown.

VARIATION

If you do not want to brown the top, arrange thinly sliced tomatoes around the edge of the dish and sprinkle the centre with freshly chopped parsley before serving.

Spinach and Feta Peppers

A mouthwatering spinach, cheese, minced beef and rice stuffing is used to fill these peppers.

Preparation time: 20 minutes
Cooking time: 22½-23½ minutes
Cals per serving: 495
Serves 4

100 g (4 oz) frozen leaf spinach, thawed	**100g (4 oz) long grain rice**
4 spring onions	**400 g (14 oz) can chopped tomatoes**
100 g (4 oz) feta cheese	**25 g (1 oz) toasted hazelnuts**
4 large red peppers, about 225 g (8 oz) each	**2.5 ml (½ tsp) freshly grated nutmeg**
	15 ml (1 tbsp) chopped fresh marjoram
15 ml (1 tbsp) oil	**salt and pepper**
300 g (11 oz) lean minced beef	**TO GARNISH**
	marjoram leaves

1 Drain and roughly chop the spinach. Chop the spring onions. Crumble the feta cheese. Cut the tops from the peppers and remove the pith and seeds.

2 Place the oil in a large microwave-proof casserole dish and cook on HIGH for 30 seconds. Stir in the lean minced beef, cover and cook on HIGH for 3 minutes. Stir after 2 minutes to break up the mince.

3 Stir in the rice and tomatoes, cover and cook on HIGH for 10 minutes.

4 Stir in the spinach, spring onions, feta, hazelnuts, nutmeg, marjoram and seasoning.

5 Pile into the peppers, replace lids if wished. Arrange peppers in a shallow dish, cover and cook on HIGH for 9-10 minutes, until tender. Serve sprinkled with marjoram leaves.

Jacket Potatoes and Fillings

Potatoes cooked in their skins in the microwave oven are ready in no time. Just add a knob of butter and plenty of seasoning, or top with one of the following fillings.

Preparation time: 5-10 minutes
Cooking time: 5-16 minutes, plus standing
Cals per potato: 235
Serves: 1-4

1-4 jacket potatoes, 175 g (6 oz) each

1 Scrub the potatoes and with a fork pierce the surface several times to prevent them bursting during cooking.

2 Place in the microwave on a double thickness of kitchen paper spaced well apart so the heat can circulate easily.

3 Cook the potatoes on HIGH, turning them over halfway through. Allow 5 minutes for 1 potato, 6-7 minutes for 2 potatoes, 12 minutes for 3 potatoes and 16 minutes for 4 potatoes. Wrap each potato in foil and leave to STAND for 5 minutes.

FILLINGS

Tandoori Chicken

Cals per potato with filling: 380

Cut two cooked potatoes in half and carefully scoop out the soft potato flesh into a bowl. Mix in 100 g (4 oz) diced cooked tandoori chicken, 45 ml (3 tbsp) mayonnaise and 15 ml (1 tbsp) chopped fresh coriander. Season well with salt and pepper. Pile the filling back into the potato shells, place them in a circle on a heatproof plate, pointing towards the centre and reheat in the microwave on HIGH for 2 minutes.

Brie and Onion

Cals per potato with filling: 340

Cut two cooked potatoes in half and carefully scoop out the soft potato flesh into a bowl. Remove the rind from 50 g (2 oz) brie and chop the cheese into small pieces. Add to the cooked potato with 3 chopped spring onions 1 egg yolk, 25 g (1 oz) butter and salt and pepper to taste. Mix together then pile the filling back into the potato shells, place them in a circle on a heatproof plate, pointing towards the centre and reheat in the microwave on HIGH for 2 minutes.

Couscous filled Aubergines

Small aubergines are an ideal vegetable to fill with a stuffing. These are served with piquant yogurt dressing.

Preparation time: 25 minutes
Cooking time: 8 minutes
Cals per serving: 170
Serves 4

2 small aubergine, about 250 g (9 oz) each	**salt and pepper**
30 ml (2 tbsp) lemon juice	**CORIANDER DRESSING**
50 g (2 oz) couscous	**1 cm (½ inch) piece fresh root ginger**
6 sun-dried tomatoes in oil	**1 garlic clove**
50 g (2 oz) no need to soak dried apricots	**150 ml (¼ pint) low fat bio yogurt**
8 fresh mint leaves	**finely grated rind and juice ½ lime**
4 spring onions	**30 ml (2 tbsp) chopped fresh coriander**
15 ml (1 tbsp) pine nuts	

1 Make the dressing: Peel and finely grate the ginger. Peel and crush the garlic. Mix together with the remaining ingredients and chill until ready to serve.

2 Cut the aubergines in half lengthways and score the cut sides deeply, without damaging the skins.

3 Arrange on a large plate and sprinkle the cut surfaces with lemon juice. Cover loosely with greaseproof paper and microwave on HIGH for 5 minutes or until slightly softened, rearranging once. Leave to stand for 5 minutes.

4 Meanwhile put the couscous in a bowl and pour on 150 ml (¼ pint) boiling water. Leave to soak and fluff up. Chop the tomatoes, apricots, mint and spring onions. Mix together with the pine nuts and seasoning.

5 Scoop the flesh out of the aubergine and chop finely. Mix with the couscous and tomato mixture. Spoon the filling into the aubergine shells. Place on a large plate, cover loosely with greaseproof paper and microwave on HIGH for 3 minutes, or until filling is hot.

6 Serve the filled aubergines with the coriander dressing.

Oriental Chicken Skewers

Strips of chicken are coated in a spicy soy sauce marinade and then speared onto wooden skewers. A piquant peanut sauce accompanies the chicken.

Preparation time: 15 minutes
Cooking time: 4-4½ minutes
Cals per serving: 390
Serves 4

400 g (14 oz) skinless chicken breast fillets	**CHILLI DIPPING SAUCE**
2.5 cm (1 inch) piece fresh root ginger	**75 g (3 oz) crunchy peanut butter**
1 garlic clove	**100 ml (4 fl oz) coconut milk**
75 ml (5 tbsp) dark soy sauce	**5 ml (1 tsp) chilli powder**
45 ml (3 tbsp) dry sherry	**30 ml (2 tbsp) dark soy sauce**
5 ml (1 tsp) ground cumin	**TO GARNISH**
5 ml (1 tsp) ground coriander	**coriander sprigs**
15 ml (1 tbsp) vegetable oil	**lime halves**

1 Slice the chicken into thick, finger length strips. Peel and grate the ginger. Peel and crush the garlic.

2 Combine the ginger, garlic, soy sauce, sherry, cumin, coriander and vegetable oil together.

3 Add the chicken and stir well to coat. Cover and refrigerate for 30 minutes. If time allows leave for 3-4 hours or even overnight.

4 Thread the chicken onto eight 12-15 cm (5-6 inch) wooden skewers. Arrange on a large microwave proof plate. Cook on HIGH for 3-3½ minutes, re-arranging after 2 minutes.

5 Meanwhile mix the dipping sauce ingredients together in a small bowl. Remove skewers from microwave and leave to stand. Cook the sauce on HIGH for 1 minute. Stir to combine.

6 Serve skewers garnished with coriander and lime. Serve with the warm peanut sauce.

DESSERTS

The versatility of the microwave oven is best demonstrated when it comes to desserts. It can be used during preparation for dissolving gelatine, melting chocolate or toasting nuts.

Fruits, both fresh and dried, cooked in the microwave keep their shape better and look more attractive than conventionally cooked fruits (see chart page 127). The variety of prepared desserts and puddings that can be cooked in the microwave is endless, ranging from light, spongy steamed suet and sponge puddings, which cook in a fraction of the time of conventionally steamed puddings, to smooth and creamy cheesecakes, which can be cooked without any concern that they may brown too much.

Sticky Date Pudding

Indulge yourself with this rich, sticky pudding, flavoured with dates and oranges. This light sponge pudding is served topped with a wonderful toffee sauce.

Preparation time: 15 minutes
Cooking time: 9 minutes, plus standing
Cals per serving: 605-460
Serves 6-8

175 g (6 oz) stoned dates	**2.5 ml (½ tsp) bicarbonate of soda**
150 ml (¼ pint) fresh orange juice	**grated rind 1 orange**
50 g (2 oz) white chocolate	**SAUCE**
75 g (3 oz) unsalted butter, softened	**125 g (4 oz) light brown muscovado sugar**
125 g (4 oz) light brown muscovado sugar	**75 g (3 oz) unsalted butter**
2 eggs	**60 ml (4 tbsp) double cream**
150 g (5 oz) self raising white flour	**15 ml (1 tbsp) lemon juice**
25 g (1 oz) cocoa powder	

1 Grease a 1.4 litre (2½ pint) pudding basin and line the base with a circle of greaseproof paper. Roughly chop the dates and place in a microwave casserole dish with the orange juice. Cover and cook on HIGH for 2 minutes. Leave to cool.

2 Roughly chop the white chocolate. Cream the butter and sugar together in a large bowl. Gradually beat in the eggs. Sift the flour, cocoa powder and bicarbonate of soda into the bowl and mix together until well blended.

3 Remove one third of the date pieces from the casserole dish and set aside. Add the remaining dates and orange juice to the pudding mixture with the orange rind and chopped chocolate. Stir well then turn into the prepared basin.

4 Cover with pierced microwave food wrap. Cook on HIGH for 5 minutes, giving the basin a half turn after 3 minutes. Leave to STAND for 5 minutes before inverting onto a serving plate. If necessary trim the top so it is level before inverting onto the serving plate.

5 Meanwhile place the sugar, butter and cream for the sauce, in a 600 ml (1 pint) jug. Cook on HIGH for 1 minute. Stir to dissolve the sugar and melt the butter. Stir in the reserved dates and lemon juice and cook on HIGH for 1 minute.

6 Pour a little sauce over the pudding and serve the remainder separately.

Jam Steamed Pudding

Gone are the days of a steamed filled kitchen and hours of cooking. The microwave oven will give a light sponge pudding in minutes. The speed has to be seen to be believed.

Preparation time: 15 minutes
Cooking time: 5 minutes, plus standing
Cals per serving: 365
Serves: 6

60 ml (4 tbsp) jam	**2 eggs**
125 g (4 oz) soft tub margarine	**15 ml (2 tbsp) milk**
125 g (4 oz) caster sugar	**TO SERVE**
125 g (4 oz) self-raising white flour	**custard or ice cream**
5 ml (1 tsp) baking powder	

1 Lightly grease a 1 litre (1¾ pint) pudding basin and place the jam in the bottom of the basin.

2 Place the margarine, caster sugar, sifted flour and baking powder into a mixing bowl with the eggs and milk.

3 Beat the ingredients together until the mixture is light and fluffy in both colour and texture.

4 Spoon the mixture into the pudding basin and cover with microwave food wrap. Microwave the pudding on HIGH for 5 minutes.

5 Leave to STAND for 2 minutes then turn onto a plate and serve with custard (see page 106) or ice cream.

VARIATIONS

Syrup Pudding: Substitute the jam with golden syrup and serve a jug of warmed syrup with the pudding when it is cooked.

Mincemeat Pudding: Line the bottom and sides of the basin with a thin layer of mincemeat and fill with the sponge mixture. When the pudding is served turn it out carefully so that the outside remains completely covered with the mincemeat.

Chocolate Pudding: Blend 60 ml (4 tbsp) cocoa powder with 30 ml (2 tbsp) hot water, then gradually beat it into the creamed mixture once all the other ingredients have been combined.

Lemon Sponge Pudding: Substitute the jam with lemon curd and add the grated rind of 1 lemon to the sponge mixture.

Peaches with Zabaglione Sauce

These tender spiced peaches are served with a warm, frothy, Marsala sauce, which is almost impossible to resist.

Preparation time: 10 minutes, plus cooling
Cooking time: 8 minutes
Cals per serving: 150
Serves 4

6 firm peaches or nectarines	**SAUCE**
5 ml (1 tsp) ground cinnamon	**1 egg**
5 ml (1 tsp) ground nutmeg	**2 egg yolks**
5 cloves	**25 g (1 oz) caster sugar**
150ml (¼ pint) orange juice	**75 ml (5 tbsp) Marsala wine**
	sprigs of lemon balm, to decorate

1 Cut the peaches in half and remove the stones. Place the peaches in a single layer around the edge of a shallow dish.

2 Mix the cinnamon, nutmeg and cloves with the orange juice and pour around the fruit. Cover and cook on HIGH for 5 minutes, or until just tender.

3 Leave to cool for about ½ hour until just warm, then prepare the sauce.

4 Place the egg, egg yolks and sugar in a large bowl and whisk until creamy.

5 Place the Marsala in a jug and cook on HIGH for 1 minute, until just boiling. Pour onto the eggs and whisk continuously. The mixture will thicken.

6 Cook on MEDIUM for 1 minute. Whisk using an electric mixer until thick and frothy. Cook on HIGH for 1 minute and whisk again briefly.

7 Remove the peaches from the dish with a slotted spoon and arrange, rounded side uppermost on individual plates. Pour the zabaglione sauce over the peaches. Decorate with lemon balm, if wished and serve immediately.

Stuffed Baked Apples

Stuffed apples make a quick warming dessert. There are three different fillings to try. All are delicious served with custard or ice cream.

Preparation time: 10 minutes
Cooking time: 7-9 minutes, plus standing
Cals per serving:
with mincemeat: 150
with date and ginger: 180
with mango and walnut: 200
Serves: 4

4 medium cooking apples	**DATE AND GINGER FILLING**
60ml (4 tbsp) golden syrup	**75 g (3 oz) dried stoned dates, chopped**
30ml (2 tbsp) lemon juice	**15 g (½ oz) crystallized stem ginger, chopped**
30ml (2 tbsp) water	**5 ml (1 tsp) grated orange rind**
MANGO AND WALNUT FILLING	**30 ml (2 tbsp) soft brown sugar**
50 g (2 oz) semi-dried mango, chopped	**MINCEMEAT FILLING**
50 g (2 oz) chopped walnuts	**60 ml (4 tbsp) mincemeat**
30 ml (2 tbsp) soft brown sugar	**30 ml (2 tbsp) soft brown sugar**

1 With the point of a sharp knife, make a slit in the skin around the middle of each apple. Core the apples.

2 Mix together the chosen stuffing ingredients and use to fill the centre of each apple.

3 Place the golden syrup, lemon juice and water in a dish large enough for the fruit to fit in one layer. Microwave on HIGH for 2 minutes or until bubbling.

4 Arrange the apples in the dish and baste with hot syrup. Cover the apples loosely with greaseproof paper and microwave on HIGH for 5-7 minutes until the fruit is just cooked, but still holds its shape. Give each apple a half turn after 3 minutes.

5 Leave to STAND, covered, for 5 minutes before serving with custard (see page 106) or ice cream.

Bread and Butter Pudding

Layers of bread and spicy dried fruits are cooked in a creamy egg custard, until it is just set. Delicious served warm.

Preparation time: 15 minutes, plus soaking
Cooking time: 10 minutes, plus standing
Cals per serving: 480
Serves: 4

50 g (2 oz) butter	**2.5 ml (½ tsp) ground cinnamon**
8 medium thick slices stale bread	**2 eggs**
50 g (2 oz) demerara sugar	**300 ml (½ pint) milk**
50 g (2 oz) sultanas	**150 ml (¼ pint) extra thick single cream**

1 Using a little of the butter, grease a 900 ml (1½ pint) shallow heatproof dish. Spread the rest of the butter over the slices of bread. Remove the crusts and cut each slice into four diagonally.

2 Reserve 15 ml (1 tbsp) demerara sugar. Mix the rest with the sultanas and cinnamon. Arrange the bread and fruit and sugar mixture in alternate layers in the dish.

3 Lightly beat the eggs together then whisk in the milk and cream. Strain the liquid into the dish, pressing the bread base down so the pieces are covered. Set aside for 30 minutes to soak.

4 Cover the pudding with microwave food wrap and cook on MEDIUM for 10 minutes or until just set. Leave to STAND for 3 minutes.

Creamy Rice Pudding

Always a popular dessert; serve on its own, with a spoonful of jam or poached fruit such as apples flavoured with cinnamon.

Preparation time: 5 minutes
Cooking time: 40 minutes, plus standing
Cals per serving: 310-205
Serves: 2-3

225 ml (8 fl oz) full cream evaporated milk	**25 g (1 oz) caster sugar**
50 g (2 oz) short-grain rice	**a little grated nutmeg**

1 Place all the ingredients with 350 ml (12 fl oz) water into a 4 litre (7 pint) buttered bowl. Mix well.

2 Cover and cook on HIGH for 5 minutes or until the liquid boils.

3 Reduce the setting to LOW and cook for 35-40 minutes or until the rice starts to thicken. Stir it with a fork every 15 minutes and also at the end of the cooking time to break up any lumps.

4 Leave the rice to STAND for 5 minutes, then sprinkle the surface with nutmeg before serving.

Chocolate Fondue

A rich chocolate sauce with double cream and orange Curaçao forms the centre of this dessert.
A selection of fruits and sweetmeats are speared onto forks and dipped into the sauce.

Preparation time: 10 minutes
Cooking time: 2½ minutes
Cals per serving: 485
Serves: 4

	TO SERVE
225 g (8 oz) plain chocolate	**fresh fruit such as apples, bananas and strawberries**
150 ml (¼ pint) double cream	**15-30 ml (1-2 tbsp) lemon juice**
30 ml (2 tbsp) orange Curaçao	**sponge fingers or Madeira cake**
	pink and white marshmallows

1 Prepare the fruit and sweetmeats for dipping. Peel, core and cut apples into chunks. Use both red and green apples for colour. Peel bananas and cut into chunks. Toss both apples and bananas in a little lemon juice to prevent discoloration. Hull the strawberries. Cut sponge fingers into four and Madeira cake into cubes. Arrange on a serving plate.

2 Break the chocolate into pieces and put it into a medium sized bowl. Microwave on HIGH for 2 minutes, stirring several times, until the chocolate melts.

3 Mix in the double cream and orange liqueur then return the bowl to the microwave and reheat the fondue on HIGH for 30 seconds, so all the ingredients are thoroughly warmed.

4 Pour the chocolate fondue mixture into a small fondue dish and stand it over a low spirit heater so the sauce remains liquid.

5 Serve with a prepared fruit, sponge and marshmallows for dipping.

Upside-Down Pear Pudding

Pear halves and cherries smothered in a sticky butter and sugar glaze nestle in the top of this
light as-air-chocolate sponge.

Preparation time: 15 minutes
Cooking time: 8½-9½ minutes, plus standing
Cals per serving: 500
Serves: 6

25 g (1 oz) butter	**125 g (4 oz) soft margarine**
25 g (1 oz) caster sugar	**125 g (4 oz) caster sugar**
410 g can pear halves in natural juice	**2 eggs**
8 glacé cherries	**90 ml (3 fl oz) milk**
SPONGE	**75 g (3 oz) white chocolate chips**
125 g (4 oz) self-raising white flour	**TO SERVE**
25 g (1 oz) cocoa powder	**Chocolate sauce**

1 Put the butter and sugar for the topping into a
20.5 cm (8 inch) straight sided heatproof dish and
microwave on HIGH for 30-40 seconds stirring once.

2 Drain the pear halves and arrange in the mixture, cut
side down with the glacé cherries in between.

3 Sift the flour and cocoa powder together. Put the
margarine, sugar, sifted flour and cocoa powder into
a mixing bowl. Beat the eggs and milk together. Add to
the mixing bowl with the white chocolate chips and stir
the ingredients together. Beat thoroughly until the mixture
is light and fluffy in texture.

4 Turn the cake mixture into the dish and carefully
spread over the fruit. Cover the dish with microwave
food wrap and cook the dessert on HIGH for 8-9 minutes
until it is well risen and feels spongy to the touch.

5 Leave to STAND for 2 minutes then ease the
pudding away from the sides of the dish and turn it
out onto a warm serving plate. Complete the dessert with
chocolate sauce (see page 106).

Raspberry and Mint Fool

The wonderful flavour of raspberries is accentuated with the addition of fresh mint in this smooth and velvety dessert.

Preparation time: 15 minutes, plus chilling
Cooking time: 4- 5 minutes
Cals per serving: 335
Serves: 6

30 ml (2 tbsp) cornflour	**50 g (2 oz) caster sugar**
300 ml (½ pint) milk	**15 ml (1 tbsp) kirsch**
450 g (1 lb) fresh or frozen raspberries	**300 ml (½ pint) double cream**
15 ml (1 tbsp) chopped fresh mint	**TO DECORATE**
	mint sprigs

1 In a large jug blend the cornflour with a little of the milk, to make a smooth paste. Stir in the remaining milk. Microwave on HIGH for 4-5 minutes, or until the sauce thickens, stirring 3-4 times.

2 Cover the surface completely with dampened grease-proof paper. Leave on one side until cold.

3 Defrost raspberries if frozen. Keeping six raspberries for decoration, sieve the rest to make a purée. Whisk the purée into the cold sauce with the chopped mint, sugar and kirsch.

4 Whip the double cream until it starts to thicken, then gradually whisk in the raspberry sauce until evenly mixed. Divide the mixture between six individual glasses and chill until required.

5 Serve each dessert decorated with a raspberry and a sprig of mint.

Crème Caramel

The microwave oven cooks this favourite dessert in less than half the time taken to cook it conventionally. The creamy vanilla custard is surrounded by a delicious rich caramel sauce .

Preparation time: 10 minutes, plus chilling
Cooking time: 21-21½ minutes, plus standing
Cals per serving: 235
Serves: 4

100g (4 oz) caster sugar	3 eggs
45 ml (3 tbsp) warm water	few drops of vanilla essence
420 ml (14 fl oz) milk	

1 Put 75 g (3 oz) of the caster sugar into a 900 ml (1½ pint) soufflé dish, stir in the warm water then microwave on HIGH for 4-4½ minutes until it caramelises to a pale golden brown. Stir the mixture occasionally if it starts to brown unevenly.

2 Stand the extremely hot dish in hot water for 2-3 minutes so the caramel stops cooking then swirl the liquid around the dish so the base and sides are just covered. Leave on one side.

3 Heat the milk in a jug on HIGH for 3 minutes. Lightly beat the eggs together, add the milk and whisk together. Add the rest of the sugar with the vanilla essence.

4 Strain the mixture into the caramel lined dish then stand the dish in a larger dish containing about 600 ml (1 pint) of hot water. The water should reach about halfway up the side of the soufflé dish.

5 Microwave the dessert, uncovered, on MEDIUM for 10 minutes. Leave to STAND for 1 minute. Cook on MEDIUM for 2 minutes, leave to STAND again for 1 minute, then cook again on MEDIUM for 2 minutes or until it is lightly set. The centre will still be soft. Leave to cool and set, still standing in the water bath.

6 Place the dessert, covered, in the refrigerator overnight to chill thoroughly. Next day turn the dessert out into a deep plate as the caramel with have dissolved and formed a delicious sauce. Serve with fresh cream if liked.

Strawberry Cheesecake

A crunchy coconut and biscuit base with a creamy vanilla cheese filling; this strawberry topped dessert is a perfect summer-time recipe.

Preparation time: 20 minutes, plus chilling
Cooking time: 13½-14½ minutes
Cals per serving: 415

Serves: 8

25 g (1 oz) desiccated coconut	**a few drops vanilla essence**
65 g (2½ oz) butter	**TOPPING**
150 g (5 oz) digestive biscuits	**7.5 ml (1½ tsp) arrowroot**
325 g (12 oz) full fat soft cheese	**15 ml (1 tbsp) caster sugar**
75 g (3 oz) caster sugar	**120 ml (4 fl oz) orange juice**
150 ml (5 fl oz) soured cream	**325 g (12 oz) strawberries**
2 eggs	

1 Sprinkle the coconut on a plate and cook on HIGH for 3-4 minutes, until toasted, stirring twice. Put the butter into a 20.5 cm (8 inch) glazed ceramic flan dish and cook on HIGH for 40 seconds, until hot and melted.

2 Crush the biscuits and stir into the butter with the coconut. Spread the mixture over the base of the dish. Return the dish to the microwave and cook on HIGH for 1 minute.

3 Beat the cheese, sugar and soured cream together. Beat in the eggs and vanilla essence. Cook on HIGH for 4 minutes, until thick, whisking every minute. Pour on top of the biscuit base and spread evenly.

4 Cook the cheesecake, uncovered on MEDIUM for 3 minutes until the edges start to set, but the centre is still soft. Leave to cool then chill for 2 hours.

5 To decorate the dessert. Blend the arrowroot in a bowl with the sugar and orange juice. Slice 50 g (2 oz) strawberries and add to the bowl. Halve the remaining strawberries and arrange on top of the cheesecake.

6 Heat the glaze on HIGH for 2-2½ minutes, until thickened, stirring once or twice during the cooking time. Pass through a sieve, to remove the strawberry pips then carefully spoon the glaze over the strawberries. Leave to set and serve chilled. Remove from the refrigerator 30 minutes before serving.

Pears in Red Wine

Whole pears are poached in a sweet red wine sauce spiced with cinnamon and cloves, which soaks into the flesh to give a wonderful flavour. Serve well chilled, scattered with toasted flaked almonds.

Preparation time: 20 minutes, plus cooling
Cooking time:18-20 minutes, plus standing
Cals per serving: 200
Serves: 6

300 ml (½ pint) red wine	**6 small, not too ripe, pears**
75 g (3 oz) caster sugar	**15 ml (1 tbsp) cornflour**
1 small cinnamon stick	**TO SERVE**
4 whole cloves	**25 g (1 oz) flaked almonds, toasted**
thinly pared rind of ½ lemon	**crème fraîche**

1 Put the wine, sugar, cinnamon stick, cloves, pared lemon rind and 150 ml (¼ pint) water into a large dish and microwave the liquid, uncovered, on HIGH for 5 minutes, stirring it once to ensure the sugar dissolves.

2 Meanwhile peel the pears, leaving them whole, and with the end of the peeler carefully remove the cores.

3 When the liquid is ready add the pears, cover and cook the fruit on HIGH for 8-10 minutes or until the fruit is just soft. Turn the pears over halfway through the cooking time so they all absorb the red wine liquid. The exact timing will depend on the ripeness of the pears.

4 Leave the fruit, still covered, to stand for 5 minutes then using a slotted spoon transfer the pears to a serving dish and keep on one side.

5 Strain the liquid, blend a little with the cornflour and when it is smooth stir in the remaining juice. Return the dish to the microwave and cook the sauce, on HIGH for 5 minutes until it thickens and clears, stirring it once.

6 Cool the sauce slightly then carefully spoon it over the pears and leave the dessert for several hours in a cool place to chill.

7 Just before serving scatter over the toasted almonds. (To toast almonds see page 13). Serve the dessert with crème fraîche.

BAKING

Cakes cooked in the microwave are light, even-textured and moist but because the sugar in them does not caramelise and form a crust on the surface they do not brown. However they rise higher than cakes baked in a conventional oven and have a more open, airy texture. Remember to only half fill the container or the mixture will overflow and create rather a mess in the microwave.

The test for a cake cooked in the microwave is the same as for a conventionally baked cake - a fine skewer inserted into the centre comes out clean. The cake may still have moist spots on the surface although the test says the cake is ready. Do not be tempted to cook the cake for a little longer, just leave it to stand when these spots should dry.

Flapjack and brownies are so quick and easy to cook in the microwave but it is impossible to make traditional crisp biscuits like gingernuts.

English Madeleines

Metal tins cannot be used in most microwave ovens, so these fun little cakes are cooked in paper cups.

Preparation time: 20 minutes, plus cooling
Cooking time: 4-6 minutes, plus standing
Cals per serving: 260
Makes: 8

100 g (4 oz) butter or margarine	**40 g (1½ oz) desiccated coconut**
100 g (4 oz) caster sugar	**TO DECORATE**
2 eggs, size 2	**4 glacé cherries**
100g (4 oz) self-raising white flour	**angelica**
75 ml (5 tbsp) red jam	

1 Grease 8 paper drinking cups. Line the base of each one with a round of greaseproof paper cut to fit.

2 Cream the butter and sugar together until very pale and fluffy. Beat the eggs together and add a little at a time, beating well after each addition. Carefully fold in the flour.

3 Divide the mixture evenly between the prepared cups. Place the cups on 2 flat heatproof plates, 4 to each plate.

4 Cover with microwave food wrap and cook one plate at a time for 1½-2 minutes until the mixture is cooked but just slightly moist on the surface. Quickly remove the microwave wrap. STAND for 1-2 minutes then carefully turn the cakes out onto a rack to cool.

5 When the cakes are almost cold, trim the bases, if necessary, so that they stand firmly and are about the same height.

6 Put the jam in a small heatproof bowl and microwave on HIGH for 1-2 minutes until melted and boiling. Sieve to remove the pips.

7 Spread the coconut out on a large plate. Spear each cake onto a fork, brush them with the hot jam then roll them in the coconut until evenly coated.

8 Cut the glacé cherries in half. Top each madeleine with half a glacé cherry and small pieces of angelica.

Rich Fruit Cake

This rich fruit cake tastes even better if left for a week to mature. If liked, decorate with walnuts and cherries, when ready to serve.

Preparation time: 15 minutes, plus cooling
Cooking time: 36-41 minutes, plus standing
Cals per slice: 375
Makes about 12 slices

2 eggs	**50 g (2 oz) glacé cherries**
100 g (4 oz) soft dark brown sugar	**700 g (1½ lb) mixed dried fruit**
30 ml (2 tbsp) black treacle	**100 g (4 oz) mixed chopped nuts**
60 ml (4 tbsp) vegetable oil	**30 ml (2 tbsp) brandy**
175 g (6 oz) self-raising white flour	**TO DECORATE**
2.5 ml (½ tsp) baking powder	**30 ml (2 tbsp) apricot jam**
5 ml (1 tsp) mixed spice	**8 walnut halves**
pinch of salt	**8 glacé cherries**
100 ml (4 fl oz) milk	

1 Base line a 20.5 cm (8 inch) round soufflé dish with greaseproof paper cut to fit.

2 In a large bowl, mix the eggs with the sugar, treacle and oil.

3 Sieve the flour, baking powder, mixed spice and salt together then stir into the mixture with the milk. Cut the cherries into quarters. Stir into the cake mix with the mixed dried fruit and nuts.

4 Spoon the mixture into the prepared dish and level the top.

5 Microwave on LOW for 35-40 minutes until a skewer inserted in the centre comes out clean.

6 Leave in the dish to STAND for 30 minutes then turn it out onto a cooling rack and leave to cool completly.

7 When cold, prick the cake with a fine skewer and pour over the brandy. Wrap in greaseproof paper and then aluminium foil. Leave to mature for about one week.

8 To decorate, put the jam into a small bowl and microwave on HIGH for 1 minute until melted. Cut the cherries in half. Spread or brush the jam over the surface of the cake and arrange the walnut and cherry halves in the centre.

Chocolate Biscuit Cake

This easy to prepare cake is made with melted chocolate, broken biscuits, sultanas, cherries and walnuts. Not only does it make a teatime treat, but is also excellent served as a dessert with whipped cream.

Preparation time: 10 minutes, plus chilling
Cooking time: 4-5 minutes
Cals per serving: 275
Makes: 10 pieces

125 g (4 oz) plain chocolate	125 g (4 oz) digestive biscuits
125 g (4 oz) butter	25 g (1 oz) glacé cherries
15 ml (1 tbsp) golden syrup	50 g (2 oz) walnuts
30 ml (2 tbsp) double cream	25 g (1 oz) sultanas

1 Grease a loose bottomed 18.5 cm (7 inch) flan dish. Break the chocolate into pieces. Cut the butter into small pieces.

2 Place the chocolate, butter, golden syrup and cream in a large bowl. Microwave on LOW for 4-5 minutes or until the chocolate has melted, stirring frequently.

3 Roughly break the biscuits. Cut the cherries into eight and roughly chop the walnuts. Add the biscuits, cherries, walnuts and sultanas to the melted chocolate and mix thoroughly.

4 Turn the mixture into the prepared flan dish and level the surface. Mark lightly into ten wedges, then chill in the refrigerator for 1-2 hours or until set.

Marmalade Cake

Chunks of orange marmalade peel are found as you bite into this tangy cake. It is also decorated with an orange icing to further enhance the orange flavour.

Preparation time: 10 minutes, plus cooling and setting
Cooking time: 5 minutes, plus standing
Cals per slice: 300
Makes 8 slices

125 g (4 oz) self-raising white flour	**75 ml (5 tbsp) chunky orange marmalade**
125 g (4 oz) softened butter or soft tub margarine	**125 g (4 oz) icing sugar**
50 g (2 oz) caster sugar	**finely grated rind of 1 orange**
2 eggs	

1 Grease a deep 20.5 cm (8 inch) round dish and line the base with greaseproof paper cut to fit.

2 Put the flour, butter or margarine, sugar, eggs and marmalade into a bowl and beat together until smooth and glossy.

3 Spoon the mixture into the dish, level the surface and cover with microwave food wrap. Stand on a microwave roasting rack and cook on HIGH for 5 minutes or until well risen and a skewer inserted into the centre comes out clean.

4 Leave, uncovered, to STAND for 5 minutes then turn out onto a wire rack, cover with a tea towel and leave to cool.

5 When the cake is cold, make the icing. Sift the icing sugar into a bowl and mix in the orange rind. Gradually add 15 ml (1 tbsp) hot water and beat together. The icing should be thick enough to coat the back of a spoon.

6 Pour the icing over the cake letting it run down the sides. Leave to set then cut into slices to serve.

Passion Cake

A tasty cake sweetened with grated carrots and chopped walnuts, it is iced with an orange flavoured cream cheese icing.

Preparation time: 15 minutes, plus cooling
Cooking time: 5 minutes, plus standing
Cals per slice: 430
Makes 10 slices

175 g (6 oz) self-raising white flour	**50 g (2 oz) chopped walnuts**
1 ml (¼ tsp) bicarbonate of soda	**ICING**
2.5 ml (½ tsp) ground cinnamon	**350 g (12 oz) medium fat cream cheese**
125 g (4 oz) light brown soft sugar	**90 ml (6 tbsp) icing sugar**
175 g (6 oz) carrots	**grated rind of 1 orange**
2 eggs	**30 ml (2 tbsp) orange juice**
150 ml (¼ pint) sunflower oil	**TO DECORATE**
5 ml (1 tsp) vanilla essence	**chopped walnuts**

1 Lightly grease a 20.5 cm (8 inch) deep soufflé dish and line the base with baking parchment.

2 Sift the flour, bicarbonate of soda and cinnamon into a bowl. Mix in the sugar. Peel and grate the carrots and mix in.

3 Beat together the eggs, oil and vanilla essence and add them to the dry ingredients. Beat together thoroughly. Fold in the walnuts.

4 Turn the mixture into the prepared dish and level the surface. Stand the dish in the microwave oven on an upturned saucer and cook on HIGH for 5 minutes, or until well risen and firm to the touch. Leave to STAND for 10 minutes.

5 Turn out onto a wire rack and leave to cool completely. Remove the paper lining.

6 Place the cream cheese in a mixing bowl. Sift in the icing sugar and beat into the cream cheese with the orange rind and juice to make a smooth icing. Cut the cake in half, spread with a thin layer of the icing and sandwich together.

7 Place the cake on a serving plate and spread the rest of the icing evenly over the top and sides of the cake leaving a rough surface. Sprinkle with chopped walnuts, to decorate.

Gingerbread

Gingerbread is always a popular cake. It is best kept for at least a day in an airtight tin for the flavours and texture to mellow. Serve sliced and spread with butter if liked.

Preparation time: 15 minutes, plus cooling
Cooking time: about 8 minutes, plus standing
Cals per slice: 155
Makes 8 slices

50 g (2 oz) margarine	**5 ml (1 tsp) ground ginger**
50 g (2 oz) dark brown soft sugar	**2.5 ml (½ tsp) ground cinnamon**
75g (3 oz) black treacle	**60 ml (4 tbsp) milk**
1 egg	**2.5 ml (½ tsp) bicarbonate of soda**
100 g (4 oz) plain white flour	

1 Using baking parchment line the base and sides of a 18.5 cm (7 inch) x 7.5 cm (3 inch) loaf shaped microwave-proof dish.

2 Put the margarine, sugar and treacle into a bowl and melt them together on HIGH for 1 minute 30 seconds, stirring once so the ingredients combine. Remove from the microwave and stir again until the ingredients are blended together.

3 Lightly beat the egg. Sift the flour, ginger and cinnamon together. Beat the egg and flour mixture into the treacle mixture. Warm the milk on HIGH for 20 seconds, mix in the bicarbonate of soda then stir the liquid into the gingerbread mixture.

4 Pour the mixture into the prepared dish and cook, uncovered on MEDIUM for 6 minutes until well risen and a cocktail stick inserted into the mixture comes out clean.

5 Leave the cake to STAND for 5 minutes then transfer it to a wire rack to cool completely.

Chocolate Loaf Cake

Golden syrup and soft dark brown sugar help to make this scrumptuous chocolate cake very moist. It is split in half and filled with whipped cream and topped with chocolate just before serving.

Preparation time: 15 minutes, plus cooling and setting
Cooking time: 8 minutes, plus standing
Cals per slice: 410
Makes 10 slices

125 g (4 oz) golden syrup	1 egg
125 g (4 oz) soft dark brown sugar	150 ml (¼ pint) milk
125 g (4 oz) butter or margarine	150ml (¼ pint) double cream
175 g (6 oz) self-raising white flour	125 g (4 oz) plain chocolate
50 g (2 oz) cocoa powder	5 ml (1 tsp) sunflower oil

1 Lightly grease a 23 cm (9 inch) loaf dish and line the base with greaseproof paper cut to fit.

2 Put the syrup, brown sugar and butter in a large bowl and microwave on HIGH for 2 minutes or until the butter has melted and the sugar dissolved, stirring occasionally.

3 Sift the flour and cocoa powder together. Mix into melted mixture. Beat in the egg and then stir in the milk.

4 Turn the mixture into the prepared dish and microwave, covered on HIGH for 5 minutes until a skewer inserted into the centre comes out clean.

5 Leave to STAND for 5 minutes then turn out onto a wire rack to cool completely.

6 Cut the cake horizontally, into 3 layers. Whip the cream until it forms soft peaks. Spread the cream over the base and middle layers of cake and sandwich the three layers together.

7 Chop the chocolate and place in a small bowl with oil. Microwave on HIGH for about 1 minute until melted, stirring occasionally. Spread the melted chocolate over the top of the cake, allowing it to trickle over the edges and sides. Leave to set.

Boston Brownies

Chocolate cakes are always popular and this recipe will be no exception. Squares of moist chocolate sponge and chewy walnuts are dusted liberally with icing sugar before serving.

Preparation time: 10 minutes, plus cooling
Cooking time: 6½-7 minutes
Cals per cake: 205
Makes: 12 squares

75 g (3 oz) plain chocolate	**2 eggs**
100 g (4 oz) butter or margarine	**2.5 ml (½ tsp) vanilla essence**
100 g (4 oz) dark brown muscovado sugar	**75 g (3 oz) walnuts**
75 g (3 oz) self-raising white flour	**sifted icing sugar, for dusting**
1.25 ml (¼ tsp) salt	

1 Grease and base line a 20.5 cm (8 inch) shallow glass ovenproof dish. Break the chocolate into pieces and dice the butter.

2 Put the chocolate and butter into a large heatproof bowl. Microwave on MEDIUM for 3 minutes until the chocolate is soft and glossy on top and the butter has melted. Stir well until smooth.

3 Stir the sugar into the chocolate mixture. Sift the flour and salt into the bowl. Add the eggs and vanilla essence and beat well to make a smooth batter. Roughly chop the walnuts and stir into the brownie mixture.

4 Pour into the prepared dish and cover with pierced microwave food wrap. Cook on HIGH for 3½-4 minutes until well risen, firm to touch and slightly moist on the surface.

5 Remove the microwave food wrap and allow the mixture to cool in the dish. Dust the cake thickly with icing sugar then cut each into 12 pieces before serving.

Coconut and Cherry Cookies

A batch of these biscuits take only a couple of minutes to cook. They are likely to be eaten almost as quickly!

Preparation time: 15 minutes, plus cooling
Cooking time: 10 minutes
Cals per biscuit: 75
Makes : 30

50 g (2 oz) glacé cherries	**2.5 ml (½ tsp) vanilla essence**
100 g (4 oz) butter or margarine	**pinch salt**
75 g (3 oz) soft dark brown sugar	**225 g (8 oz) plain white flour**
1 egg	**50 g (2 oz) desiccated coconut**
30 ml (2 tbsp) milk	**icing sugar, for dusting**
10 ml (2 tsp) baking powder	

1 Chop the glacé cherries. Put the butter and sugar into a bowl and beat together until very soft and fluffy. Beat in the egg, then stir in the remaining ingredients.

2 Line a large round plate or microwave baking tray with baking parchment. Drop 6 heaped teaspoonfuls of dough in a circle on the tray, spacing them apart.

3 Cook on HIGH for 2 minutes or until the surface of the biscuits look dry. Allow the biscuits to cool slightly on the baking tray, then transfer them to a wire rack to cool completely.

4 Repeat with the remaining mixture. Dust with icing sugar and serve. Store for up to two days in an air-tight container.

Chewy Flapjacks

These chewy biscuits are made from porridge oats sweetened with golden syrup and dark brown sugar. They have a spicy cinnamon flavour.

Preparation time: 10 minutes, plus cooling
Cooking time: 5½ minutes
Cals per biscuit: 205
Makes: 8

75 g (3 oz) margarine	**150 g (5 oz) porridge oats**
100 g (4 oz) golden syrup	**5 ml (1 tsp) ground cinnamon**
50 g (2 oz) dark brown soft sugar	

1 Place the margarine, syrup and sugar into a 20.5 cm (8 inch) shallow heatproof glass dish and cook the ingredients on HIGH for 2 minutes stirring once or twice until they have melted and are blended together.

2 Mix in the porridge oats and cinnamon and when the ingredients are well combined spread the mixture level in the dish. Clean the sides of the dish.

3 Return the dish to the oven and cook, uncovered, on HIGH for 3½ minutes. The mixture will bubble up to almost twice its depth whilst it is cooking.

4 Leave the flapjacks to cool for 10 minutes then mark into 8 pieces. When almost cold cut through the marks and transfer the biscuits to wire rack to cool completely. Store in an airtight tin until required.

Quick Rolls

If you run short of bread, or have some unexpected guests, these quick rolls can be made in minutes. They do not keep, so are best eaten whilst still warm from the oven.

Preparation time: 15 minutes
Cooking time: 4 minutes
Cals per roll: 125
Makes : 10 rolls

125 g (4 oz) plain white flour	**25 g (1 oz) butter or margarine**
100 g (4 oz) plain wholemeal flour	**about 150 ml (¼ pint) milk**
10 ml (2 tsp) baking powder	**45 ml (3 tbsp) coarse oatmeal or cracked wheat**
2.5 ml (½ tsp) salt	

1 Put the flours, baking powder and salt into a large bowl. Rub in the butter until evenly distributed.

2 Make a well in the centre, add the milk and mix with a round-bladed knife to give a fairly soft dough. Add a little extra milk if necessary.

3 Turn the mixture onto a floured board and divide it into ten pieces and shape each into a roll.

4 Flatten the top of each roll then brush with water and sprinkle with the coarse oatmeal or cracked wheat.

5 Place the rolls around the edge of two large flat plates, five to a plate. Microwave one plate at a time on HIGH for 2 minutes or until risen.

6 Cool on a wire cooling rack. The rolls are best eaten while still warm.

SAUCES, PRESERVES AND CONFECTIONERY

The versatility of the microwave is yet again demonstrated in this chapter. A wide variety of sauces both sweet and savoury can be made in the microwave. Always remember to use a large enough container to prevent the sauce boiling over, as it increases in bulk as it boils. Also stir the sauce often to prevent lumps forming, especially if it is a flour based sauce.

For small amounts of jams and chutneys the microwave is ideal and the results are excellent. For chutney makers there is the added bonus that the house will not smell of vinegar for days afterwards.

Finally sweets couldn't be more simple than when cooked in the microwave oven. The task is also very safe as containers of hot, bubbling syrups are safe behind the closed door of the microwave oven. Again as with sauces remember to use a large container in which to cook the mixture, as it at least doubles in bulk as it boils.

Custard Sauce

Once you have made custard in the microwave oven you will never return to stirring the sauce constantly on a hot stove.

Preparation time: 3 minutes
Cooking time: 3-4 minutes
Calories per serving: 155
Serve 4

15-30 ml (1-2 tbsp) sugar	**600 ml (1 pint) milk**
45 ml (3 tbsp) custard powder	

1 Blend the sugar and custard powder together with a little of the milk in a large measuring jug. Gradually stir in the remaining milk.

2 Microwave the sauce on HIGH for 3-4 minutes or until thickened, stirring after every minute to ensure the sauce is smooth. Stir well and serve.

Chocolate Sauce

This luxurious sauce is the ultimate for chocolate lovers. It is delicious with hot sponge puddings or poured over ice cream.

Preparation time: 5 minutes
Cooking time: 4 minutes
Calories per serving: 355
Serves 2

100 g (4 oz) plain chocolate	**10 ml (2 tsp) sunflower oil**
25 g (1 oz) caster sugar	

1 Measure 150 ml (¼ pint) cold water. Put the chocolate, sugar, oil and 10 ml (2 tsp) from the cold water into a heatproof jug about 1 litre (1¾ pint) capacity.

2 Heat the ingredients together on HIGH for 1 minute, stirring once, so they are blended.

3 Mix in the remaining water and microwave uncovered on HIGH for 3 minutes, until the sauce has thickened slightly, stirring once. As the sauce cooks it will rise up in the jug.

4 Stir the sauce thoroughly when cooked then serve either hot or cold as required.

Barbecue Sauce

A strong and spicy sauce, perfect for serving with grilled meats.

Preparation time: 5 minutes
Cooking time: 10-11 minutes
Cals per serving: 140
Serves: 4

50 g (2 oz) butter or margarine	**30 ml (2 tbsp) demerara sugar**
1 medium onion	**10 ml (2 tsp) mustard powder**
15 ml (1 tbsp) tomato purée	**30 ml (2 tbsp) Worcestershire sauce**
30 ml (2 tbsp) malt vinegar	

1 Put the butter into a medium heatproof bowl. Microwave on HIGH for 1 minute until melted. Peel and chop the onion. Stir into the butter, cover and microwave on HIGH for 4-5 minutes until softened.

2 Whisk all the remaining ingredients together with 150 ml (¼ pint) water then stir into the onion. Microwave, uncovered, on HIGH for 5 minutes stirring frequently. Serve hot.

Hollandaise Sauce

A classic sauce which is easier to make in the microwave oven.

Preparation time: 5 minutes
Cooking time: 3½ minutes
Cals per serving: 215
Serves 4

4 tbsp white wine vinegar	**125 g (4 oz) butter**
6 peppercorns	**2 egg yolks**
1 small bay leaf	**salt and pepper**

1 Put the vinegar, peppercorns and bay leaf into a 600 ml (1 pint) heatproof bowl. Heat uncovered on HIGH for 1½ minutes. Remove the peppercorns and bay leaf. Cut the butter into small pieces and add to the bowl. Microwave on HIGH, uncovered for 1½ minutes or until melted.

2 Add the egg yolks and whisk the sauce for 1-2 minutes until it is thick and creamy. Reheat the sauce, uncovered on HIGH for 30 seconds, whisk and check for seasoning before serving. It is ready when thick enough to coat the back of a spoon.

Lemon Curd

This mouthwatering preserve is less likely to curdle, made in the microwave.

Preparation time: 10 minutes
Cooking time: 7 minutes
Cals per 15 ml (1 tbsp): 35
Makes 900 g (2 lb)

finely grated rind and juice 4 large lemons	**225 g (8 oz) caster sugar**
4 eggs	**125 g (4 oz) butter**

1 Put the lemon rind into a heatproof bowl. Mix the lemon juice and eggs together and strain the liquid into the bowl. Stir in the sugar and then add the butter.

2 Cover the bowl with microwave food wrap and cook the mixture on HIGH for 1 minute.

3 Remove the wrap, stir the mixture and return the bowl, uncovered, to the microwave and cook on MEDIUM for 6 minutes until the lemon curd thickens. Whisk well every minute, to prevent curdling.

4 Using oven gloves, remove the bowl from the oven and continue whisking until the mixture cools. The lemon curd will thicken on cooling.

5 Pour the lemon curd into sterilised jars. (See page 13). Cover and label. Store in the refrigerator for up to 3 weeks.

Orange Marmalade

The microwave really comes into its own when making small amounts of preserves as it cuts the cooking time by half, compared to the conventional method.

Preparation time: 20 minutes, plus cooling
Cooking time: 30-35 minutes
Calories per 15 ml (1 tbsp): 45
Makes: 1.4 kg (3 lbs)

675 g (1½ lb) Seville oranges	**1 kg (2.2 lb) bag granulated sugar**
1 large lemon	**knob of butter**
600 ml (1 pint) water	

1 Squeeze the juice from both the oranges and the lemon and put into a large mixing bowl. Scrape the inside of the fruit shells clean, removing excess pith as well.

2 Put the insides of the fruit shells into a piece of muslin and tie it up.

3 Shred the peel finely and add the pieces to the bowl with the muslin bag and the water. Cover the bowl and microwave the fruit on HIGH for 15 minutes or until the pieces of peel are soft.

4 Remove the muslin bag when it is cool enough to handle and squeeze out all the moisture from it back into the bowl.

5 Stir the sugar into the liquid and when it has almost dissolved return the bowl to the microwave and cook the marmalade, uncovered, on HIGH for 15-20 minutes until set.

6 Stir in the butter then leave the marmalade for 15 minutes to cool-this helps to keep the peel pieces evenly distributed through the preserve.

7 Pour the marmalade into hot sterilised jars (See page 13). Cover and label then store in a cool, dark place until required.

Raspberry Jam

This recipe uses frozen fruit, so is ideal to make any time of the year. Make in the depth of winter and you can taste the full flavours of summer fruits.

Preparation time: 5 minutes, plus cooling
Cooking time: 20 minutes
Cals per 15 ml (1 tbsp): 40
Makes: 700 g (1½ lb)

450 g (1 lb) frozen raspberries	**450 g (1 lb) granulated sugar**
30 ml (2 tbsp) lemon juice	**knob of butter**

1 Put the frozen raspberries in a large heatproof bowl and microwave on HIGH for 3 minutes to thaw. Stir the fruit several times with a wooden spoon to ensure even thawing.

2 Add the lemon juice and sugar. Mix well and microwave on HIGH for 5 minutes until the sugar has dissolved. Stir several times during cooking.

3 Add the butter and microwave on HIGH for 12 minutes, stirring occasionally, until setting point is reached. Remove any scum with a slotted spoon.

4 Leave to cool for 15 minutes to prevent the fruit rising in the jars. Pour into hot sterilised jars, (see page 13), cover and label, then store in a cool dark place until required.

Strawberry Jam

The best loved of all home-made jams. Nothing can beat an afternoon tea of warm scones topped with butter and freshly made strawberry jam.

Preparation time: 10 minutes, plus cooling
Cooking time: 17-20 minutes
Cals per 15 ml (1 tbsp): 40
Makes : 700 g (1½ lb)

450 g (1 lb) fresh strawberries	**450 g (1 lb) granulated sugar**
juice of 1 lemon	**knob of butter**

1 Hull, wash and drain the strawberries and put them into a large heatproof bowl with the lemon juice. Cover the bowl and microwave the fruit on HIGH for 5 minutes so it starts to soften, stirring it once or twice.

2 Mash the fruit slightly then stir in the sugar and when it has almost dissolved return the bowl to the microwave and cook the jam uncovered on HIGH for 12-15 minutes or until setting point is reached.

3 Stir the jam occasionally as it cooks to ensure the sugar has completely dissolved.

4 Stir in the butter then leave the jam to cool for 15 minutes to prevent the fruit from rising in the jars. Pour into hot sterilised jars, (see page 13), cover and label then store in a cool dark place until required.

Mango Chutney

Mango chutney is a wonderful accompaniment to serve with curries, with cold meats and cheese.

Preparation time: 15 minutes
Cooking time: 25 minutes
Cals per 15 ml (1 tbsp): 15
Makes about 800g (1¾ lb)

3 large mangoes	**125 g (4 oz) light brown soft sugar**
2.5 cm (1 inch) piece of fresh root ginger	**200 ml (7 fl oz) distilled or cider vinegar**
1 small red chilli	**2.5 ml (½ tsp) ground ginger**
1 garlic clove	

1 Peel the mangoes and cut the flesh away from the stone. Chop the flesh into small pieces.

2 Peel and finely chop the ginger. Cut the chilli in half, remove the seeds and chop the flesh. Peel and crush the garlic. Place the mango, ginger, chilli, garlic, sugar, vinegar and ground ginger in a large heatproof bowl.

3 Microwave on HIGH for 5 minutes, or until the sugar has dissolved, stirring occasionally. Microwave on HIGH for 20 minutes, or until thick and well reduced. Stir two to three times during cooking.

4 Leave for 5 minutes to cool slightly, turn into sterilised jars (see page 13), cover with polythene, label and store in a dry dark place for at least 4 weeks to mature.

Date and Apple Chutney

A tasty apple, onion, date and sultana chutney. As with all chutneys, the flavour develops on storing.

Preparation time: 20 minutes
Cooking time: 25 minutes
Cals per 15 ml (1 tbsp): 20
Makes: 1.5 kg (3 lb)

450 g (1 lb) cooking apples	**225 g (8 oz) light brown soft sugar**
1 large onion	**5 ml (1 tsp) ground ginger**
1 garlic clove	**5 ml (1 tsp) ground cinnamon**
225 g (8 oz) dates	**300 ml (½ pint) malt vinegar**
125 g (4 oz) sultanas	

1 Peel, core and chop the apples. Peel and chop the onion. Peel and crush the garlic. Chop the dates.

2 Put the apples, onion, garlic, dates, sultanas, sugar, ginger and cinnamon into a large bowl. Stir in the vinegar and cover the bowl with microwave food wrap.

3 Cook on HIGH for 15 minutes, stirring the mixture several times. Remove the cover and cook for a further 10 minutes.

4 Leave to cool slightly then spoon the chutney into warm, sterilised jars (see page 13). Cover with polythene, label and store in a dry, dark place for about 6 weeks before using to allow the flavours to mature.

Tomato Chutney

Tomatoes, apples, onions and sultanas mixed with ginger, cayenne pepper and a hint of mustard make this perfect chutney to serve with cheese.

Preparation time: 20 minutes
Cooking time: 48 minutes, plus standing
Cals per 15 ml (1 tbsp): 15
Makes: 900 g (2 lb)

700 g (1½ lb) firm tomatoes	**5 ml (1 tsp) salt**
225 g (8 oz) cooking apples	**200 ml (7 fl oz) malt vinegar**
1 medium onion	**15g (½ oz) ground ginger**
125 g (4 oz) soft dark brown sugar	**1.25 ml (¼ tsp) cayenne pepper**
125 g (4 oz) sultanas	**2.5 ml (½ tsp) mustard powder**

1 Put the tomatoes in a large heatproof bowl and just cover with boiling water. Microwave on HIGH for 3 minutes, then transfer the tomatoes to cold water and remove the skins.

2 Peel, core and chop the apples. Peel the onion and quarter. Blend the apples and onion to a thick paste in a food processor. Roughly chop the tomatoes.

3 Mix the tomatoes, apples and onion, sugar, sultanas, salt, vinegar, ginger, cayenne and mustard powder together in a large heatproof bowl.

4 Cover and microwave on HIGH for 45 minutes until the mixture is thick and has no excess liquid. Stir every 5 minutes during cooking and take particular care, stirring more frequently during the last 5 minutes.

5 Leave to STAND for 10 minutes then stir. Pour into hot sterilised jars, (see page 13), cover and label and store for 4 weeks before using so the flavours develop.

Coconut Ice

Pink and white squares of sugary coconut, that appeal to all ages. Keeps well in an airtight tin.

Preparation time: 5 minutes, plus setting
Cooking time: 12-13 minutes
Cals per piece: 115
Makes about 24 pieces

450 g (1 lb) granulated sugar	**150g (5 oz) desiccated coconut**
150 ml (¼ pint) milk	**a little cochineal colouring**

1 Stir the sugar and milk together in a 4 litre (7 pint) heatproof bowl and heat on HIGH for 5 minutes stirring the mixture twice so the sugar dissolves.

2 Once every grain has melted cook the syrup on HIGH for 2 minutes and then on MEDIUM for 5-6 minutes or until a small amount dropped into a cup of cold water forms a soft ball (116°C, 240°F).

3 Beat in the coconut then turn half the mixture into a shallow, lightly greased, 18 cm (7 inch) square tin and spread it level.

4 Quickly colour the remaining mixture pink with the cochineal and spread it over the white base.

5 Leave the coconut ice to cool then cut into 24 pieces with a sharp knife and transfer to small sweet cases.

Butter Tablet

There are several variations of this fudgy butter tablet to make. With the bubbling sugar syrup, shut in the microwave oven it is a safer way for children to help make sweets.

Preparation time: 5 minutes, plus cooling
Cooking time: 10 minutes
Cals per piece: 50
Makes: 36 pieces

300 g (10 oz) caster sugar	**50 g (2 oz) butter**
170 g can evaporated milk	**2.5 ml (½ tsp) vanilla essence**
50 ml (2 fl oz) milk	

1 Put the sugar, evaporated milk and milk into a very large heatproof bowl - when the mixture boils initially it quadruples in capacity - and stir together.

2 Cut the butter into pieces, and add to the bowl. Microwave the mixture on HIGH for 10 minutes stirring it once halfway through the cooking time to ensure the sugar has dissolved properly.

3 Check if the fudge is ready by dropping a small amount into a glass of cold water. If the mixture forms a soft ball it is ready. If not return the bowl to the microwave and cook for 1 more minute before testing again.

4 When the mixture is ready, add the vanilla essence and beat it well for about 3 minutes or until it starts to thicken.

5 Pour into a lightly greased 15 cm (6 inch) square tin and leave to cool for 5 minutes then mark into pieces.

6 Cut through the marks when completely cold and store in an airtight container until required.

VARIATIONS

Chocolate: Stir in 125 g (4 oz) grated plain chocolate with the vanilla essence.

Coffee: Add 15 ml (1 tbsp) liquid coffee to the mixture with the evaporated milk.

Praline

This mixture of caramelised nuts and sugar is ideal for flavouring sauces, sprinkling over ice cream, or to decorate desserts.

Preparation time: 5 minutes, plus cooling
Cooking time: 8-9 minutes
Cals per 15 ml (1 tbsp): 75
Makes about 100 g (4 oz)

---

50 g (2 oz) blanched almonds

50 g (2 oz) granulated sugar

---

1 Put the almonds onto a heatproof plate and cook on HIGH for 3-4 minutes turning them often until the nuts are golden brown. Leave on one side.

2 Put the sugar and 30 ml (2 tbsp) water into a 1 litre (1¾ pint) heatproof bowl. Stir together then microwave uncovered on HIGH for 5 minutes or until the mixture starts to caramelise.

3 Stir in the nuts then quickly turn the praline onto a greased baking tray and leave to cool and harden.

4 To crush the praline cover it with a piece of paper and using a rolling pin break it into fine crumbs. Alternatively the praline can be crushed in a food processor, but break it up slightly by hand before placing it in the machine.

5 Store the praline in an airtight container until required. It is delicious as a flavouring for butter cream for cakes or it can be added to vanilla ice cream.

THAWING MEAT

Frozen meat exudes a lot of liquid during thawing and because microwaves are attracted to water, the liquid should be poured off or mopped up with absorbent kitchen paper when it collects, otherwise thawing will take longer. Start thawing a joint in its wrapper and remove it as soon as possible – usually after one-quarter of the thawing time. Place the joint on a microwave roasting rack so that it does not stand in liquid during thawing.

Remember to turn over a large piece of meat. If the joint shows signs of cooking give the meat a 'rest' period of 20 minutes. A joint is thawed when a skewer can easily pass through the thickest part of the meat. Chops and steaks should be re-positioned during thawing; test them by pressing the surface with your fingers – the meat should feel cold to the touch and give in the thickest part.

Type	Time on DEFROST Setting	Notes
BEEF		
Boned roasting joints (sirloin, topside)	8–10 minutes per 450 g (1 lb)	Turn over regularly during thawing and rest if the meat shows signs of cooking. Stand for 1 hour.
Joints on bone (rib of beef)	10–12 minutes per 450 g (1 lb)	Turn over joint during thawing. The meat will still be icy in the centre but will complete thawing if you leave to stand for 1 hour.
Minced beef	8–10 minutes per 450 g (1 lb)	Break up with a fork during thawing. Stand for 10 minutes.
Cubed steak	6–8 minutes per 450 g (1 lb)	Stand for 10 minutes.
Steak (sirloin, rump)	8–10 minutes per 450 g (1 lb)	Stand for 10 minutes.
LAMB/VEAL		
Boned rolled joint (loin, leg, shoulder)	5–6 minutes per 450 g (1 lb)	As for boned roasting joints of beef above. Stand for 30–45 minutes.
On the bone (leg and shoulder)	5–6 minutes per 450 g (1 lb)	As for beef joints on bone above. Stand for 30–45 minutes.
Minced lamb or veal	8–10 minutes per 450 g (1 lb)	As for minced beef. Stand for 10 minutes.
Chops	8–10 minutes per 450 g (1 lb)	Separate during thawing. Stand for 10 minutes.
PORK		
Boned rolled joint (loin leg)	7–8 minutes per 450 g (1 lb)	As for boned roasting joints of beef above. Stand for 1 hour.
On the bone (leg, hand)	7–8 minutes per 450 g (1 lb)	As for beef joints on bone above. Stand for 1 hour.
Tenderloin	8–10 minutes per 450 g (1 lb)	Stand for 10 minutes.

Type	Time on DEFROST setting	Notes
Chops	8–10 minutes per 450 g (1 lb)	Separate during thawing and arrange 'spoke' fashion. Stand for 10 minutes.
OFFAL		
Liver	8–10 minutes per 450 g (1 lb)	Separate during thawing. Stand for 5 minutes.
Kidney	6–9 minutes per 450 g (1 lb)	Separate during thawing. Stand for 5 minutes.

COOKING MEAT

Type	Time/Setting	Microwave Cooking Technique(s)
BEEF		

Boned roasting joints (sirloin, topside)	per 450 g (1 lb)
	Rare: 4–5 minutes on HIGH
	Medium: 3–4 minutes on HIGH
	  3–4 minutes on MEDIUM
	Well done: 4–5 minutes on HIGH
	  4–5 minutes on MEDIUM
		Turn over joint halfway through cooking time.
		Stand for 15–20 minutes, tented in foil.

On the bone roasting joint (fore rib, back rib)	per 450 g (1 lb)
	Rare: 4 minutes on HIGH
	Medium: 2 minutes on HIGH
	  3 minutes on MEDIUM
	Well done: 3 minutes on HIGH
	  4 minutes on MEDIUM
		Turn over joint halfway through cooking time.
		Stand as for boned joint.

LAMB/VEAL		

Boned rolled joint (loin, leg, shoulder)	per 450 g (1 lb)
	Medium: 3–4 minutes on HIGH
	  3–4 minutes on MEDIUM
	Well done: 4–5 minutes on HIGH
	  4–5 minutes on MEDIUM
		Turn over joint halfway through cooking time.
		Stand as for beef.

On the bone (leg and shoulder)	per 450 g (1 lb)
	Medium: 3 minutes on HIGH
	  4 minutes on MEDIUM
	Well done: 4 minutes on HIGH
	  5 minutes on MEDIUM
		Position fatty side down and turn over halfway through cooking time.
		Stand as for beef.

Chops	1 chop: 2–3 minutes on HIGH 2 chops: 3–4 minutes on HIGH 3 chops: 4–5 minutes on HIGH 4 chops: 5–6 minutes on HIGH	Cook in preheated browning dish. Position with bone ends towards centre. Turn over once during cooking.
BACON		
Joints	12–14 minutes on MEDIUM per 450 g (1 lb)	Cook in a pierced roasting bag. Turn over joint partway through cooking time. Stand for 10 minutes, tented in foil.
Rashers	2 rashers: 2 minutes on HIGH 4 rashers: 4 minutes on HIGH 6 rashers: 5 minutes on HIGH	Arrange in a single layer. Cover with greaseproof paper to prevent splattering. Cook in a preheated browning dish if liked. Remove paper immediately after cooking to prevent sticking.

Type	Time/Setting	Microwave Cooking Technique(s)
PORK		
Boned rolled joint (loin, leg)	per 450 g (lb) 4 minutes on HIGH 5 minutes on MEDIUM	As for boned rolled lamb above.
On the bone (leg, hand)	4 minutes on HIGH 4 minutes on MEDIUM	As for lamb on the bone above.
Chops	1 chop: 4 minutes on HIGH 2 chops: 5 minutes on HIGH 3 chops: 6 minutes on HIGH 4 chops: 6½ minutes on HIGH	Cook in preheated browning dish. Prick kidney, if attached. Position with bone ends towards centre. Turn over once during cooking.
OFFAL		
Liver (lamb and calves)	6 minutes on HIGH per 450 g (1 lb)	Cover with greaseproof paper to prevent splattering.
Kidneys	6 minutes on HIGH per 450 g (1 lb)	Arrange in a circle. Cover to prevent splattering. Re-position during cooking.

THAWING POULTRY AND GAME

Poultry or game should be thawed in its freezer wrapping, which should be pierced first and the metal tag removed. During thawing, pour off liquid that collects in the bag. Finish thawing in a bowl of cold water with the bird still in its bag. Chicken portions can be thawed in their polystyrene trays.

Type	Time on DEFROST Setting	Notes
Whole chicken or duckling.	6–8 minutes per 450 g (1 lb)	Remove giblets. Stand in cold water for 30 minutes.
Whole turkey	10–12 minutes per 450 g (1 lb)	Remove giblets. Stand in cold water 2–3 hours.
Chicken portions	5–7 minutes per 450 g (1 lb)	Stand for 10 minutes.
Poussin, grouse, pheasant, pigeon, quail	5–7 minutes per 450 g (1 lb)	

COOKING POULTRY

Type	Time/Setting	Microwave Cooking Technique(s)
CHICKEN		
Whole chicken	8 minutes on MEDIUM per 450 g (1 lb)	Cook in a roasting bag, breast side down, and turn halfway through cooking. Stand for 10–15 minutes.
Portions	6 minutes on HIGH per 450 g (1 lb)	Position skin side up with thinner parts towards the centre. Re-position halfway through cooking time. Stand for 5–10 minutes.
Boneless breast	2–3 minutes on HIGH	

Type	Time/Setting	Microwave Cooking Technique(s)
DUCK		
Whole	7 minutes on MEDIUM per 450 g (1 lb)	Turn over as for whole chicken. Stand for 10–15 minutes.
Portions	4 x 300 g (11 oz) pieces: 5 minutes on HIGH, then 30 minutes on MEDIUM	Position and re-position as for portions above.
TURKEY		
Whole	9–11 minutes on MEDIUM per 450 g (1 lb)	Turn over three or four times, depending on size, during cooking; start cooking breast side down. Stand for 10–15 minutes.

THAWING FISH AND SHELLFISH

Separate cutlets, fillets or steaks as soon as possible during thawing, and remove pieces from the microwave as soon as they are thawed. Timing will depend on the thickness of the fish.

Type	Time/Setting	Notes
Whole round fish (mullet, trout, carp, bream, whiting)	4–6 minutes per 450 g (1 lb) on DEFROST	Stand for 5 minutes after each 2–3 minutes. Very large fish are thawed more successfully if left to stand for 10–15 minutes after every 2–3 minutes.
White fish fillets or cutlets (cod, coley, haddock, halibut, monkfish, whole plaice or sole)	3–4 minutes per 450 g (1 lb) on DEFROST	Stand for 5 minutes after each 2–3 minutes.
Lobster, crab, crab claws	6–8 minutes per 450 g (1 lb) on DEFROST	Stand for 5 minutes after each 2–3 minutes.
Crab meat	4–6 minutes per 450 g (1 lb) block on DEFROST	Stand for 5 minutes after each 2–3 minutes.
Prawns, shrimps, scampi, scallops	2–3 minutes per 100 g (4 oz) 3–4 minutes per 225 g (8 oz) on DEFROST	Arrange in a circle on a double sheet of absorbent kitchen paper to absorb liquid. Separate during thawing with a fork and remove pieces from cooker as they thaw.

COOKING FISH AND SHELLFISH

The cooking time depends on the thickness of the fish as well as the amount being cooked and whether it is cooked whole, in fillets or cut up into smaller pieces. This chart is a guide only. Always check before the end of the calculated cooking time to prevent overcooking. Simply put the fish in a single layer in a shallow dish with 30 ml (2 tbsp) stock, wine, milk or water per 450 g (1 lb) of fish (unless otherwise stated), then cover and cook as below.

Type	Time/Setting	Microwave Cooking Technique(s)
Whole round fish (whiting, mullet, trout, carp, bream, small haddock)	4 minutes on HIGH per 450 g (1 lb)	Slash skin to prevent bursting. Turn fish over halfway through cooking time if fish weighs more than 1.4 kg (3 lb). Re-position fish if cooking more than two.
Whole flat fish (plaice, sole)	3 minutes on HIGH per 450 g (1 lb)	Slash skin. Check fish after 2 minutes.

Type	Time/Setting	Microwave Cooking Technique(s)
Cutlets, steaks, thick fish fillets (cod, coley, haddock, halibut, monkfish fillet)	4 minutes on HIGH per 450 g (1 lb)	Position thicker parts towards the outside of the dish. Turn halfway through cooking if steaks are very thick.
Flat fish fillets (plaice, sole)	2–3 minutes on HIGH per 450 g (1 lb)	Check fish after 2 minutes.
Dense fish fillets, cutlets, steaks. (tuna, swordfish, conger eel) whole monkfish tail	5–6 minutes on HIGH per 450 g (1 lb)	Position thicker parts towards the outside of the dish. Turn halfway through cooking if thick.
Skate wings	6–7 minutes on HIGH per 450 g (1 lb)	Add 150 ml (¼ pint) stock or milk. Cook more than 900 g (2 lb) in batches.
Smoked fish	Cook as appropriate for type of fish, e.g. whole fillet or cutlet. See above.	
Squid	Put prepared squid, cut into rings, in a large bowl with 150 ml (¼ pint) wine, stock or water per 450 g (1 lb) of squid. Cook, covered, on HIGH for 4–6 minutes per 450 g (1 lb).	Time depends on size of squid – larger, older squid are tougher and may take longer to cook.
Octopus	Put prepared octopus, cut into 2.5 cm (1 inch) pieces, in a large bowl with 150 ml (¼ pint) wine, stock or water per 450 g (1 lb) of octopus. Cook covered, on HIGH until liquid is boiling, then on MEDIUM for 15–20 minutes per 450 g (1 lb).	Tenderize octopus before cooking by beating vigorously with a meat mallet or rolling pin. Marinate before cooking to help tenderize. Time depends on age and size of octopus.
Scallops (shelled)	2–4 minutes on high per 450 g (1 lb)	Do not overcook or scallops will be tough. Add corals for 1–2 minutes at end of cooking time.
Scallops in their shells	Do not cook in the microwave.	Cook conventionally.
Mussels	Put up to 900 g (2 lb) mussels in a large bowl with 150 ml (¼ pint) wine, stock or water. Cook, covered, on HIGH for 3–5 minutes.	Remove mussels on the top as they cook. Shake the bowl occasionally during cooking. Discard any mussels that do not open.
Oysters	Do not cook in the microwave.	Cook conventionally.
Raw prawns	2–5 minutes on HIGH per 450 g (1 lb), stirring frequently.	Time depends on the size of the prawns. Cook until colour changes to bright pink.
Cockles	Put cockles in a large bowl with a little water. Cook, covered, on HIGH for 3–4 minutes until the shells open. Take cockles out of their shells and cook for a further 2–3 minutes or until hot.	Shake the bowl occasionally during cooking.
Live lobster	Do not cook in the microwave.	Cook conventionally.
Live crab	Do not cook in the microwave.	Cook conventionally.
Small clams	Cook as mussels	As mussels.
Large clams	Do not cook in the microwave	Cook conventionally.

THAWING BAKED GOODS AND PASTRY

To absorb the moisture of thawing cakes, breads and pastry, place them on absorbent kitchen paper (remove as soon as thawed to prevent sticking). For greater crispness, place baked goods and the paper on a microwave rack to allow the air to circulate underneath.

Type	Quantity	Time on DEFROST Setting	Notes
Loaf, whole **Loaf, whole**	1 large 1 small	6-8 minutes 4–6 minutes	Uncover and place on absorbent kitchen paper. Turn over during thawing. Stand for 5–15 minutes.
Loaf, sliced **Loaf, sliced**	1 large 1 small	6-8 minutes 4–6 minutes	Thaw in original wrapper but remove any metal tags. Stand for 10–15 minutes.
Slice of bread	25 g (1 oz)	10–15 seconds	Place on absorbent kitchen paper. Time carefully. Stand for 1-2 minutes.
Bread rolls, tea-cakes, scones, crumpets etc.	2 4	15–20 seconds 25–35 seconds	Place on absorbent kitchen paper. Time carefully. Stand for 2-3 minutes

CAKES AND PASTRIES

Cakes

	2 small	30–60 seconds	Place on absorbent kitchen paper. Stand for 5 minutes.
	4 small	1–1½ minutes	
Sponge cake			
	450 g (1 lb)	1–1½ minutes	Place on absorbent kitchen paper. Test and turn after 1 minute. Stand for 5 minutes.
Jam doughnuts			
	2	45–60 seconds	
	4	45–90 seconds	
Cream doughnuts			
	2	45–60 seconds	Place on absorbent kitchen paper. Stand for 10 minutes.
	4	1¼–1¾ minutes	
Cream éclairs			
	2	45 seconds	Stand for 5-10 minutes.
	4	1–1½ minutes	Stand for 15-20 minutes.
Choux buns			
	4 small	1–1½ minutes	Stand for 20-30 minutes.

PASTRY

Shortcrust and puff

	227 g (8 oz) packet	1 minute	Stand for 20 minutes.
	397 g (14 oz) packet	2 minutes	Stand for 20–30 minutes.

COOKING FROZEN VEGETABLES

Frozen vegetables may be cooked straight from the freezer. Many may be cooked in their original plastic packaging, as long as it is first slit and then placed on a plate. Alternatively, transfer to a bowl.

Vegetable	Quantity	Time on HIGH Setting	Microwave Cooking Technique(s)
Asparagus	275 g (10 oz)	6–8 minutes	Separate and re-arrange after 3 minutes.
Beans, broad	225 g (8 oz)	6–7 minutes	Stir or shake during cooking period.
Beans, green cut	225 g (8 oz)	5–7 minutes	Stir or shake during cooking period.
Broccoli	275 g (10 oz)	6–8 minutes	Re-arrange spears after 3 minutes.
Brussels sprouts	225 g (8 oz)	5–7 minutes	Stir or shake during cooking period.
Cauliflower florets	275 g (10 oz)	6–8 minutes	Stir or shake during cooking period.
Carrots	225 g (8 oz)	5–6 minutes	Stir or shake during cooking period.
Corn-on-the-cob	1 2	3–4 minutes 6–7 minutes	Do not add water. Dot with butter, wrap in greaseproof paper. Place in dish.
Mixed vegetables	225 g (8 oz)	4–5 minutes	Stir or shake during cooking period.
Peas	225 g (8 oz)	4–5 minutes	Stir or shake during cooking period.
Peas and carrots	225 g (8 oz)	6–7 minutes	Stir or shake during cooking period.
Spinach, leaf or chopped	275 g (10 oz)	6–8 minutes	Do not add water. Stir or shake during cooking period.
Swede and Turnip, diced	225 g (8 oz)	5–6 minutes	Stir or shake during cooking period. Mash with butter after standing time.
Sweetcorn	225 g (8 oz)	4–5 minutes	Stir or shake during cooking period.

COOKING FRESH VEGETABLES

When using this chart add 60 ml (4 tbsp) water unless otherwise stated. The vegetables can be cooked in boil-in-the-bags, plastic containers and polythene bags – pierce the bag before cooking to make sure there is a space for the steam to escape.

Prepare vegetables in the normal way. It is most important that food is cut to an even size and stems are of the same length. Vegetables with skins, such as aubergines, need to be pierced before cooking to prevent bursting.

Season vegetables with salt after cooking if required. Salt distorts the microwave patterns and dries the vegetables.

Vegetable	Quantity	Time on HIGH Setting	Microwave Cooking Technique(s)
Artichoke	1 2 3 4	4–5 minutes 6–7 minutes 10–11 minutes 11–12 minutes	Place upright in a covered dish.
Asparagus	450 g (1 lb)	6–7 minutes	Place stalks towards the outside of the dish. Re-position during cooking.
Aubergine	450 g (1 lb) 5 mm (¼ inch) slices	5–6 minutes	Stir or shake after 4 minutes.
Beans, broad	450 g (1 lb)	6–8 minutes	Stir or shake after 3 minutes and test after 5 minutes.
Beans, green	450 g (1 lb) sliced into 2.5 cm (1 inch) lengths	10–13 minutes	Stir or shake during the cooking period. Time will vary with age.
Beetroot, whole	4 medium	12–15 minutes	Pierce skin with a fork. Re-position during cooking.
Broccoli	450 g (1 lb) small florets	7-8 minutes	Re-position during cooking. Place stalks towards the outside of the dish.
Brussel sprouts	225 g (8 oz) 450 g (1 lb)	4–6 minutes 7–10 minutes	Stir or shake during cooking.
Cabbage	450 g (1 lb) quartered 450 g (1 lb) shredded	8 minutes 8–10 minutes	Stir or shake during cooking.
Carrots	450 g (1 lb) small whole 450 g (1 lb) 5 mm (¼ inch) slices	8–10 minutes 9–12 minutes	Stir or shake during cooking.
Cauliflower	whole 450 g (1 lb) 225 g (8 oz) florets 450 g (1 lb) florets	9–12 minutes 5–6 minutes 7–8 minutes	Stir or shake during cooking.
Celery	450 g (1 lb) sliced into 2.5 cm (1 inch) lengths	8–10 minutes	Stir or shake during cooking.
Corn-on-the-cob	2 cobs 450 g (1 lb)	6–7 minutes	Wrap individually in greased greaseproof paper. Do not add water. Place in a dish. Turn over after 3 minutes.

Type	Quantity	Time on HIGH Setting	Microwave Cooking Technique(s)
Courgettes	450 g (1 lb) 2.5 cm (1 inch) slices	5–7 minutes	Add 30 ml (2 tbsp) water. Stir or shake twice during cooking. Stand for 2 minutes.
Fennel	450 g (1 lb) 5 mm (¼ inch) slices	7–9 minutes	Stir and shake during cooking.
Leeks	450 g (1 lb) 2.5 cm (1 inch) slices	6–8 minutes	Stir or shake during cooking.
Mangetouts	450 g (1 lb)	6–8 minutes	Stir or shake during cooking.
Mushrooms	225 g (8 oz) whole 450 g (1 lb) whole	2–3 minutes 5 minutes	Do not add water. Add 25 g (1 oz) butter or alternative fat and a squeeze of lemon juice. Stir or shake gently during cooking.
Onions	225 g (8 oz) thinly sliced 450 g (1 lb) small whole	7–8 minutes 9–11 minutes	Stir or shake sliced onions. Add only 60 ml (4 tbsp) water to whole onions. Re-position whole onions during cooking.
Okra	450 g (1 lb) whole	6–8 minutes	Stir or shake during cooking.
Parsnips	450 g (1 lb) halved	10–16 minutes	Place thinner parts towards centre. Add a knob of butter and 15 ml (1 tbsp) lemon juice with 150 ml (¼ pint) water. Turn dish during cooking and re-position.
Peas	450 g (1 lb)	9–11 minutes	Stir or shake during cooking.
Potatoes, baked jacket	1 x 175 g (6 oz) potato 2 x 175 g (6 oz) potatoes 4 x 175 g (6 oz) potatoes	4–6 minutes 6–8 minutes 12–14 minutes	Prick the skin with a fork. Place on absorbent kitchen paper. Arrange more than two in a circle. Turn over halfway through cooking time.
Potatoes, boiled (old) halved	450 g (1 lb)	7–10 minutes	Stir or shake during cooking.
Potatoes, boiled (new) whole	450 g (1 lb)	6–9 minutes	
Sweet potatoes	450 g (1 lb)	5 minutes	
Spinach	450 g (1 lb) chopped	5–6 minutes	Do not add water. Best cooked in roasting bag, sealed with non-metal fastening.
Swede	450 g (1 lb) 2 cm (¾ inch) dice	11–13 minutes	Stir or shake during cooking.
Turnip	450 g (1 lb) 2 cm (¾ inch) dice	9–11 minutes	Stir or shake during cooking.

COOKING PASTA AND RICE

Put the pasta or rice and salt to taste in a large bowl. Pour over enough boiling water to cover the pasta or rice by 2.5 cm (1 inch). Stir and cover then cook on HIGH for the stated time, stirring occasionally.

Note: Large quantities of pasta and rice are better cooked conventionally.

Type and Quantity	Time on HIGH Setting	Microwave Cooking Technique(s)
Fresh white/wholemeal/spinach pasta 225 g (8 oz)	3–4 minutes	Stand for 5 minutes. Do not drain.
Dried white/wholemeal/spinach pasta shapes 225 g (8 oz)	8–10 minutes	Stand for 5 minutes. Do not drain.
Dried white/wholemeal/spinach pasta shapes 450 g (1 lb)	12–14 minutes	Stand for 5 minutes. Do not drain.
Dried white/wholemeal spaghetti 225 g (8 oz)	7–8 minutes	Stand for 5 minutes. Do not drain.
Dried white/wholemeal spaghetti 450 g (1 lb)	8–10 minutes	Stand for 5 minutes. Do not drain.
Brown rice 225 g (8 oz)	30–35 minutes	Rinse grains before cooking. Stand for 5 minutes.
Brown rice 100 g (4 oz)	25–30 minutes	Rinse grains before cooking. Stand for 5 minutes
White rice 225 g (8 oz)	10–12 minutes	Rinse grains before cooking. Stand for 5 minutes.
White rice 100 g (4 oz)	8–10 minutes	Rinse grains before cooking. Stand for 5

COOKING PULSES

The following pulses will cook successfully in the microwave oven, making considerable time savings on conventional cooking. However, pulses with very tough skins, such as red kidney beans, black beans, butter beans, cannellini beans, haricot beans and soya beans will not cook in less time and are better if cooked conventionally. Large quantities of all pulses are best cooked conventionally.

All pulses double in weight when cooked, so if a recipe states 225 g (8 oz) cooked beans, you will need to start with 110 g (4 oz) dried weight.

Soak beans overnight, then drain and cover with enough boiling water to come about 2.5 cm (1 inch) above the level of the beans. Cover and cook on HIGH for the time stated below, stirring occasionally.

Type	Time on HIGH Setting	Microwave Cooking Technique(s)
225 g (8 oz) quantity		
Aduki beans	30–35 minutes	Stand for 5 minutes. Do not drain.
Black-eye beans	25–30 minutes	Stand for 5 minutes. Do not drain.
Chick peas	50–55 minutes	Stand for 5 minutes. Do not drain.
Flageolet beans	40–45 minutes	Stand for 5 minutes. Do not drain.

Type	Time on HIGH Setting	Microwave Cooking Technique(s)
Mung beans	30–35 minutes	Stand for 5 minutes. Do not drain.
Split peas/lentils	25–30 minutes	No need to soak overnight. Stand for 5 minutes. Do not drain.

COOKING FRESH AND DRIED FRUIT

When using this chart add 15–30 ml (1–2 tbsp) water to every 450 g (1 lb) fruit to be cooked unless otherwise stated. The fruit should be cooked in a covered, microwave proof container with a vent for steam to escape.

Prepare the fruit in the normal way. It is important that it is cut into even-sized pieces. Stir the fruit once during cooking unless otherwise stated. Add sugar to taste when cooked so it can dissolve during the 5 minutes 'standing' time.

Quantity/Fruit	Time on HIGH Setting	Microwave Cooking Technique(s)
Apples 450 g (1 lb)	6–8 minutes	Peel core and slice.
Apricots (fresh) 450 g (1 lb)	5 minutes	Halve and stone.
(dried) 225 g (½ lb)	25–30 minutes	Add 600 ml (1 pint) water. No need to soak. Stir several times.
Blackberries 450 g (1 lb)	4–5 minutes	Sort over.
Blackcurrants 225 g (½ lb)	4–5 minutes	Strip from stems.
Gooseberries 450 g (1 lb)	4–5 minutes	Top and tail.
Pears 450 g (1 lb)	8–10 minutes	Peel, core and quarter. Add 150 ml (¼ pint) water.
Plums (fresh) 450 g (1 lb)	4-5 minutes	Halve and stone.
Prunes 225 g (½ lb)	18–20 minutes	Add 450 ml (¾ pint) water. No need to soak. Stir several times.
Rhubarb 450 g (1 lb)	4–5 minutes	Cut into 2.5 cm (1 inch) lengths.

Index